C++ Unleashed: High-Performance Coding and Modern Best Practices Master

C++ *for competitive programming, game development, and software engineering*

THOMPSON CARTER

Table of Content

TABLE OF CONTENTS

Introduction

C++ is one of the most powerful and versatile programming languages, widely used in a variety of domains, from system programming to game development, embedded systems, and high-performance applications. Its ability to combine low-level system access with high-level abstractions makes it an indispensable tool for developers working in performance-critical environments. Whether you are building sophisticated software systems, creating high-speed applications, or optimizing resource usage, mastering C++ can open doors to solving complex problems with efficiency and precision.

This book, **C++ Unleashed: High-Performance Coding and Modern Best Practices**, is designed to help you navigate the vast landscape of C++ programming, from its fundamental concepts to advanced techniques that allow you to write modern, maintainable, and high-performance code. Whether you are a beginner just starting with C++ or an experienced developer looking to deepen your understanding of the language, this book will provide you with the tools, knowledge, and techniques needed to master C++.

Why C++?

C++ has stood the test of time due to its unique combination of power and flexibility. It provides the ability to write high-performance applications while allowing developers to manage memory manually, offering a level of control that many modern programming languages lack. C++ is widely used in performance-sensitive areas like:

- **Game development**: C++ is the backbone of major game engines such as Unreal Engine and is used to develop AAA games with intricate physics and graphics.
- **System programming**: Operating systems, drivers, and system utilities rely heavily on C++ to interact directly with hardware and manage system resources.
- **High-performance computing**: C++'s ability to optimize for both time and space makes it ideal for computationally intense fields such as scientific computing, machine learning, and financial applications.

- **Embedded systems**: C++ is a go-to language for embedded systems, where hardware constraints demand fine-grained control over resources.

Despite being one of the older languages, C++ continues to evolve, introducing features that modernize the language and make it easier to use. C++20 introduced powerful features such as **concepts**, **ranges**, **coroutines**, and much more, ensuring that C++ remains relevant in modern development environments.

What This Book Covers

This book is structured to provide a comprehensive guide to mastering C++ for both new and experienced developers. It covers the full breadth of C++ programming, starting with the foundational aspects and progressing to more advanced topics. Here is an outline of the journey this book will take you on:

1. **Foundational Concepts**: For those new to C++ or programming, we start with an introduction to the language's syntax, core concepts, and essential features such as variables, data types, functions, and control structures. We'll also explore memory

management and the basics of object-oriented programming (OOP).

2. **Advanced C++ Features**: As you become more comfortable with C++, we dive into more complex topics such as **templates, smart pointers**, and **advanced OOP principles** like polymorphism, inheritance, and operator overloading. We will also cover powerful new features from **C++20** that enhance the language's capabilities.

3. **High-Performance Programming**: C++ is often chosen for its ability to handle performance-critical applications. This book delves deeply into how to optimize your code for both speed and memory usage, exploring techniques like **multithreading, memory management, profiling**, and **performance tuning**.

4. **Cross-Platform Development**: Modern C++ applications must run across different platforms. This book covers the best practices for writing **cross-platform C++ code**, making your applications work on Windows, Linux, and macOS, while also addressing **platform-specific issues**.

5. **Real-World Projects**: To demonstrate how C++ is applied in real-world scenarios, this book takes you

through projects such as building a **game engine**, creating a **high-performance database engine**, and working with an **existing large C++ codebase**. These examples give you the tools you need to approach and solve real-world software development challenges.

6. **Best Practices**: Writing maintainable, efficient, and error-free C++ code is critical. This book highlights best practices for **code readability, error handling, unit testing, debugging**, and **working with modern development tools** like **IDEs, build systems**, and **version control**.

7. **Future Trends**: Finally, we will discuss the future of C++ development, including upcoming features in **C++23** and beyond, as well as the role of C++ in emerging fields like **machine learning** and **web development**.

How to Use This Book

This book is structured in a way that allows you to read through it sequentially or reference it as needed. If you are new to C++, you should follow the chapters in order to build a strong foundation and gradually move on to more complex

topics. For experienced developers, the chapters on
advanced topics, performance optimization, and real-world
project examples can serve as a reference to solve specific
challenges in your current projects.

Throughout this book, you will find practical examples, code
snippets, and exercises to help you solidify your
understanding. The examples are designed to be clear and
simple, yet powerful enough to demonstrate core concepts
and advanced techniques. You will also be introduced to a
variety of C++ libraries and tools that will help you work
efficiently in modern development environments.

Who This Book is For

This book is aimed at a wide range of readers, including:

- **Beginner programmers** who are new to C++ or
  object-oriented programming.
- **Intermediate C++ developers** looking to strengthen
  their skills and learn more advanced techniques.
- **Experienced developers** who want to stay updated
  on modern C++ features, performance optimization,
  and best practices for writing maintainable, cross-
  platform code.

- **Software engineers** working in fields like game development, system programming, high-performance computing, or embedded systems.

Why C++?

C++ is a language that has endured through decades of rapid technological advancement, and its continued evolution ensures it remains relevant in modern software development. It's a language that gives you the control you need to build powerful, high-performance applications while still supporting modern programming paradigms like **object-oriented programming**, **generic programming**, and **functional programming**.

Mastering C++ will open doors to numerous opportunities in industries where performance, efficiency, and control are paramount. This book provides you with a deep dive into the language, equipping you with the knowledge and practical skills needed to build robust, high-performance software.

In the following chapters, you will gain a solid understanding of C++'s core features, advanced concepts, performance optimizations, and real-world applications. By the end of this book, you will be able to confidently write modern C++ code, harness its full potential, and tackle complex software engineering challenges with ease.

Welcome to **C++ Unleashed**. Let's begin the journey of mastering one of the most powerful and versatile programming languages in existence today!

CHAPTER 1

INTRODUCTION TO C++ AND HIGH-PERFORMANCE CODING

1.1 Overview of C++ and its Significance in High-Performance Applications

C++ is one of the most powerful and widely used programming languages, known for its flexibility, efficiency, and speed. It was designed with system programming and performance-intensive applications in mind, making it ideal for high-performance tasks like competitive programming, game development, and software engineering. C++ offers a unique blend of low-level memory control and high-level abstraction, which allows developers to optimize code for both time and space.

The language is particularly important in contexts where execution speed and efficient resource usage are critical. For example:

- **Game development**: C++ is used to write real-time game engines and graphics programming. Its performance capabilities enable smooth graphics rendering and complex game logic.

- **System programming**: C++ gives programmers access to hardware resources, making it a go-to language for writing operating systems, device drivers, and embedded systems.

- **Competitive programming**: The language's ability to handle large inputs and outputs quickly, coupled with efficient algorithm design, makes it popular among competitive programmers.

Through its support for object-oriented programming (OOP), data abstraction, and low-level memory manipulation, C++ provides the tools necessary for achieving high-performance results in various domains.

1.2 History and Evolution of C++

C++ was created by Bjarne Stroustrup in 1979 at Bell Labs. It started as an enhancement to the C programming language, which itself was developed in the 1970s and became widely adopted due to its efficiency and low-level access to hardware. Stroustrup's aim was to add object-oriented programming features to C while maintaining its high-performance characteristics.

The first major version, called "C with Classes," introduced classes and objects, which allowed for encapsulation and abstraction. By 1985, the language had evolved into C++ and included support for other object-oriented concepts like inheritance and polymorphism.

Over the years, C++ has continued to evolve, with several versions released:

- **C++98**: The first standardized version of C++, including improvements to the standard library and syntax.
- **C++03**: A minor revision focused on fixing issues and clarifying certain language features.
- **C++11**: A major update, introducing modern features like auto keyword, nullptr, and lambda functions.
- **C++14 and C++17**: These versions continued refining language features, improving performance and usability.
- **C++20**: Added more powerful features like concepts, ranges, and modules, further improving the language's expressiveness.

C++ has always strived to keep a balance between low-level memory control and high-level abstractions, making it suitable for a wide variety of applications, from embedded systems to large-scale software development.

1.3 Setting Up the Development Environment

To get started with C++, setting up a proper development environment is crucial. The steps below will guide you through setting up a basic environment for both Windows and Unix-based systems:

1.3.1 Installing the Compiler

- **Windows**: The most popular compiler for Windows is **MinGW** (Minimalist GNU for Windows). You can install it via the **MSYS2** or **Code::Blocks** IDE for an easier setup, or use **Microsoft Visual Studio** which comes with its own C++ compiler.
  - Download MinGW from the official website or use the MSYS2 package manager.
  - If using Visual Studio, download the community edition from Microsoft's site, which includes a full C++ environment.
- **MacOS**: C++ comes pre-installed with **Xcode** (Apple's IDE), and it includes a C++ compiler (Clang).
  - Install Xcode via the Mac App Store and use its command-line tools with `xcode-select --install`.

- **Linux**: Most Linux distributions come with **GCC** (GNU Compiler Collection), which includes a C++ compiler.
    - o Install GCC using the package manager: `sudo apt-get install build-essential` for Ubuntu or `sudo yum groupinstall "Development Tools"` for Fedora.

1.3.2 Setting Up an IDE

Integrated Development Environments (IDEs) provide a range of tools that can help manage your C++ code more efficiently:

- **Visual Studio Code**: Lightweight and highly customizable, this IDE supports C++ with various extensions like the C++ extension from Microsoft.
- **CLion**: A more comprehensive option for C++ development, providing powerful code analysis, refactoring tools, and debugging capabilities.
- **Code::Blocks**: A free, open-source IDE that supports C++ development with a simple interface, suitable for beginners.

1.3.3 Building Your First C++ Program

Once the tools are set up, you can create your first C++ program. Open a text editor or IDE, create a new file called `main.cpp`, and add the following code:

cpp

```cpp
#include <iostream>

int main() {
    std::cout << "Hello, World!" << std::endl;
    return 0;
}
```

To compile the program:

- **Windows (MinGW)**: Run `g++ main.cpp -o hello.exe` from the terminal and execute it by typing `./hello.exe`.
- **Mac/Linux**: Use the command `g++ main.cpp -o hello` and run it using `./hello`.

This simple example introduces you to the basic structure of C++ programs:

- `#include <iostream>`: Includes the necessary library for input and output.
- `main()`: The entry point of a C++ program.
- `std::cout`: Used to print output to the console.
- `return 0;`: Signals successful program termination.

1.4 Basic Syntax and Structure of C++

C++ has a straightforward syntax that can be learned progressively. Here are some fundamental building blocks of C++:

1.4.1 Variables and Data Types

Variables in C++ are declared with a specific data type, which determines the kind of data they can store. Common data types include:

- **int**: Integer numbers.
- **float**: Floating-point numbers (decimal values).
- **char**: Character data type (e.g., 'A').
- **bool**: Boolean values (`true` or `false`).

Example:

cpp

```cpp
int age = 25;
float salary = 50000.50;
char grade = 'A';
bool isStudent = true;
```

1.4.2 Functions

Functions allow you to group code into reusable blocks. In C++, functions are declared with a return type, a name, and a parameter list.

Example:

cpp

```cpp
int add(int a, int b) {
    return a + b;
}
```

1.4.3 Control Flow

Control flow statements such as if, else, and loops (for, while) help control the flow of the program based on conditions.

Example:

cpp

```cpp
if (age > 18) {
```

```
    std::cout << "Adult";
} else {
    std::cout << "Minor";
}
```

This chapter provides the necessary foundation to start coding in C++ and prepares you for more advanced topics. As you move forward, you'll learn to master the nuances of C++ and apply them in real-world high-performance applications.

4o mini

You said:

Chapter 2: Understanding Data Types and Memory Management • Primitive and user-defined data types • Pointers, references, and memory management • Dynamic memory allocation and deallocation • Common pitfalls in memory handling

ChatGPT said:

Chapter 2: Understanding Data Types and Memory Management

2.1 Primitive and User-Defined Data Types

In C++, data types define the kind of data that can be stored and manipulated within a program. They determine how much space a variable occupies in memory and the type of operations that can be performed on the data.

2.1.1 Primitive Data Types

Primitive data types are built into the language and represent basic values. Here are some common primitive data types in C++:

- **int**: Represents integer values (whole numbers). Example: `int age = 25;`
- **float**: Represents floating-point numbers (decimal values). Example: `float salary = 50000.75;`
- **double**: Similar to `float`, but with double the precision. Example: `double pi = 3.14159;`
- **char**: Represents a single character or symbol. Example: `char grade = 'A';`
- **bool**: Represents a boolean value (`true` or `false`). Example: `bool isActive = true;`
- **wchar_t**: Represents wide characters (used for international text). Example: `wchar_t symbol = L'あ';`

2.1.2 User-Defined Data Types

User-defined data types allow programmers to create complex data structures to represent real-world entities. C++ provides several ways to define new types:

- **Structs**: Used to define collections of variables (called members) that can hold different data types.

  Example:

  cpp

  ```cpp
  struct Person {
      std::string name;
      int age;
  };
  Person person1 = {"Alice", 30};
  ```

- **Classes**: Similar to structs, but with additional features like methods (functions), private/protected members, and constructors.

  Example:

  cpp

  ```cpp
  class Car {
  ```

```cpp
public:
    std::string make;
    int year;
    void start() {
        std::cout << "Car started" <<
std::endl;
    }
};
Car car1 = {"Toyota", 2020};
```

- **Enums**: Define a set of named integer constants, making code more readable.

  Example:

  cpp

  ```cpp
  enum Day { Monday, Tuesday, Wednesday,
  Thursday, Friday };
  Day today = Wednesday;
  ```

- **Typedefs (and aliasing with using)**: Used to create alternative names for existing data types.

  Example:

  cpp

  ```cpp
  typedef unsigned long ulong;
  ```

```
ulong population = 7800000000;
// Or using the modern aliasing approach
using byte = unsigned char;
```

2.2 Pointers, References, and Memory Management

C++ gives developers fine-grained control over memory, which allows for efficient management but also introduces potential risks. Understanding pointers, references, and memory management is crucial in avoiding bugs and optimizing performance.

2.2.1 Pointers

A pointer is a variable that stores the memory address of another variable. Pointers are often used for dynamic memory allocation and passing large structures or arrays efficiently to functions.

- **Pointer Declaration**: To declare a pointer, use the * symbol.

  Example:

  cpp

  ```
  int num = 10;
  ```

25

```cpp
int* ptr = &num; // Pointer to an integer,
holds the address of num
```

- **Dereferencing a Pointer**: Access the value stored at the memory address the pointer is pointing to by using the * operator.

Example:

cpp

```cpp
std::cout << *ptr; // Output: 10
```

- **Null Pointer**: A pointer that does not point to any valid memory address.

Example:

cpp

```cpp
int* ptr = nullptr;
```

2.2.2 References

A reference is an alias for another variable. It doesn't require dereferencing and is often used in function arguments to avoid ing large data structures.

- **Reference Declaration**: To declare a reference, use the & symbol.

  Example:

  cpp

  ```
  int num = 10;
  int& ref = num; // ref is now another name
  for num
  ref = 20; // num is now 20
  ```

- **Reference vs. Pointer**:
  - o A pointer can be reassigned to point to a different address, but a reference must always refer to the same variable.
  - o Dereferencing a pointer is required, while references don't require dereferencing.

2.2.3 Memory Management

Memory management is one of the most powerful and potentially dangerous aspects of C++. It involves allocating memory dynamically (at runtime) and releasing it when it's no longer needed.

- **Stack vs. Heap Memory**:

- o **Stack**: Memory that is automatically managed for local variables. It's faster but limited in size.
- o **Heap**: Memory that is manually managed via dynamic allocation. It is much larger but requires careful handling to avoid memory leaks.

- **Memory Allocation**:
  - o **Static Allocation**: Occurs at compile time, and the memory size is fixed.

Example:

cpp

```
int arr[5]; // Fixed-size array, memory
allocated at compile time
```

  - o **Dynamic Allocation**: Occurs at runtime, using the new keyword. Memory must be manually freed using delete.

Example:

cpp

```
int* ptr = new int; // Allocating memory
for one integer
*ptr = 10;
delete ptr; // Freeing the allocated memory
```

For arrays:

cpp

```cpp
int* arr = new int[5]; // Allocating memory
for an array of 5 integers
delete[] arr; // Freeing the array memory
```

2.3 Dynamic Memory Allocation and Deallocation

Dynamic memory allocation allows for flexible use of memory, allocating space for objects during runtime. This is particularly useful when you don't know the amount of memory needed in advance, like for handling variable-sized input data.

2.3.1 Allocating Memory with new

The new keyword is used to allocate memory dynamically on the heap. You can use it for single variables or arrays.

- **Single Variable Allocation**:

cpp

```cpp
int* ptr = new int(10); // Allocates memory
for an integer and assigns it 10
```

- **Array Allocation**:

29

```cpp
int* arr = new int[5]; // Allocates memory
for 5 integers
```

2.3.2 Deallocating Memory with `delete`

Memory that is allocated with `new` must be manually deallocated using `delete`. Failing to do so leads to memory leaks, which can cause your program to consume excessive memory over time.

- **Single Variable Deallocation**:

```cpp
delete ptr; // Frees memory allocated for
a single variable
```

- **Array Deallocation**:

```cpp
delete[] arr; // Frees memory allocated for
an array
```

2.4 Common Pitfalls in Memory Handling

While C++ gives you power over memory, it also requires discipline and attention to detail. Here are some common pitfalls in memory handling:

2.4.1 Memory Leaks

Memory leaks occur when dynamically allocated memory is not freed, leading to wasted memory that cannot be reused. This can cause your program to crash or slow down over time. Always ensure that every `new` is paired with a `delete`, and every `new[]` with `delete[]`.

2.4.2 Dangling Pointers

A dangling pointer is a pointer that continues to point to memory that has already been deallocated. Dereferencing a dangling pointer leads to undefined behavior.

- **Example:**

cpp

```
int* ptr = new int(10);
delete ptr;
// ptr is now a dangling pointer
```

31

To avoid this, always set the pointer to `nullptr` after
deleting:

cpp

```
delete ptr;
ptr = nullptr;
```

2.4.3 Double Deletion

Double deletion happens when you try to delete a pointer
that has already been deleted. This causes undefined
behavior and can crash your program. To prevent this,
always check if a pointer is `nullptr` before deleting it.

- **Example**:

    cpp

    ```
    delete ptr;
    delete ptr; // Error: double delete
    ```

2.4.4 Buffer Overflow

Buffer overflows occur when a program writes more data to
a block of memory than it can hold. This can corrupt data
and lead to crashes. Always ensure that you don't exceed the
bounds of arrays or dynamically allocated memory.

Conclusion

In this chapter, we covered the basics of C++ data types, memory management, and pointers. Understanding these fundamental concepts is crucial for writing high-performance and reliable C++ applications. By avoiding common pitfalls like memory leaks, dangling pointers, and double deletion, you can write more robust code that runs efficiently and safely.

CHAPTER 3

CONTROL STRUCTURES AND FUNCTIONS

3.1 Conditionals and Loops

Control structures are the backbone of program flow in C++. They allow you to make decisions and repeat actions based on conditions. In C++, the primary control structures are conditionals (if-else) and loops (for, while, do-while).

3.1.1 Conditionals

Conditionals allow you to execute specific blocks of code depending on whether a given condition is true or false. The most common conditional statements in C++ are `if`, `else if`, and `else`.

- **Basic `if` statement:**

  ```cpp
  int age = 20;
  if (age >= 18) {
      std::cout << "Adult" << std::endl;
  ```

34

```
}
```

- **`else if` and `else` for multiple conditions**:

cpp

```cpp
int age = 20;
if (age < 13) {
    std::cout << "Child" << std::endl;
} else if (age < 18) {
    std::cout << "Teenager" << std::endl;
} else {
    std::cout << "Adult" << std::endl;
}
```

- **Ternary Operator**: A shorthand version of an `if-else` statement.

cpp

```cpp
int age = 20;
std::cout << (age >= 18 ? "Adult" : "Not
Adult") << std::endl;
```

3.1.2 Loops

Loops allow you to execute a block of code repeatedly. The main types of loops in C++ are `for`, `while`, and `do-while`.

- **For loop**: Best used when the number of iterations is known beforehand.

cpp

```cpp
for (int i = 0; i < 5; i++) {
    std::cout << "Iteration " << i << std::endl;
}
```

- **While loop**: Useful when you want to loop until a certain condition is met, but you don't know the exact number of iterations.

cpp

```cpp
int i = 0;
while (i < 5) {
    std::cout << "Iteration " << i << std::endl;
    i++;
}
```

- **Do-while loop**: Similar to the `while` loop, but ensures that the block of code executes at least once.

cpp

```cpp
int i = 0;
do {
    std::cout << "Iteration " << i <<
std::endl;
    i++;
} while (i < 5);
```

3.1.3 Break and Continue

Both `break` and `continue` are used to control the flow of loops:

- **break**: Terminates the loop completely.

cpp

```cpp
for (int i = 0; i < 10; i++) {
    if (i == 5) {
        break;  // Exits the loop when i
equals 5
    }
    std::cout << i << " ";
}
```

- **continue**: Skips the current iteration and continues with the next iteration of the loop.

cpp

```cpp
for (int i = 0; i < 10; i++) {
    if (i == 5) {
        continue;  // Skips printing 5
    }
    std::cout << i << " ";
}
```

3.2 Writing Efficient Functions

Functions are a fundamental part of any C++ program, enabling you to break the program into reusable pieces of code. Writing efficient functions is crucial for both code readability and performance.

3.2.1 Function Basics

A function is defined by specifying its return type, name, and parameters (if any). Here's a simple example:

cpp

```cpp
int add(int a, int b) {
    return a + b;
}
```

- **Return Type**: The data type that the function will return (e.g., int, float).
- **Function Name**: A descriptive name for the function.

- **Parameters**: Input values for the function. These are optional.

3.2.2 Best Practices for Writing Efficient Functions

- **Minimize global variables**: Limit the use of global variables within functions to ensure modular and reusable code.
- **Pass by reference**: If you need to modify a large object or pass an object without ing it, pass it by reference rather than by value.

cpp

```cpp
void modifyValue(int& value) {
    value = 100;  // Modifies the original value
}
```

- **Avoid unnecessary copies**: When passing large objects like arrays or classes, use references to avoid ing large amounts of data.

cpp

```cpp
void            processLargeData(const
std::vector<int>& data) {
```

```
    // Use data without making a
}
```

- **Avoid deep nesting**: Deeply nested functions can be difficult to read and maintain. Try to flatten the logic for easier debugging.
- **Return early**: Return from a function as soon as possible if the result is determined. This helps to avoid unnecessary computations.

cpp

```cpp
int findMax(int a, int b) {
    if (a > b) return a;
    return b;
}
```

3.3 Recursion vs. Iteration

Recursion and iteration are two different approaches to solving problems in programming. While both are valid, choosing the right one can have a significant impact on performance and clarity.

3.3.1 Recursion

Recursion is when a function calls itself to solve a problem. It's particularly useful for problems that can be broken down

into smaller subproblems of the same type (e.g., calculating
factorials, traversing tree structures).

- **Example: Factorial Calculation Using Recursion**:

cpp

```cpp
int factorial(int n) {
    if (n <= 1) {
        return 1; // Base case
    }
    return n * factorial(n - 1); //
Recursive call
}
```

- **Pros**:
    - Elegant and easier to write for problems like tree
      traversal and divide-and-conquer algorithms.
    - Code is often cleaner and more concise.
- **Cons**:
    - Can lead to a stack overflow if the recursion depth
      is too large (e.g., with large inputs).
    - Performance may be slower due to repeated
      function calls and the overhead of managing the
      call stack.

3.3.2 Iteration

Iteration involves repeating a block of code using loops. It's often more efficient in terms of performance since it avoids the overhead of function calls.

- **Example: Factorial Calculation Using Iteration**:

  cpp

  ```cpp
  int factorial(int n) {
      int result = 1;
      for (int i = 1; i <= n; i++) {
          result *= i;
      }
      return result;
  }
  ```

- **Pros**:
  - More efficient in terms of memory and processing speed, as it avoids the function call stack overhead.
  - Suitable for problems where the number of iterations is known ahead of time or the problem doesn't fit the recursive pattern.
- **Cons**:

    o   Can lead to more complex code for problems that
naturally fit a recursive approach.

3.3.3 Choosing Between Recursion and Iteration

- Use **recursion** for problems like depth-first searches, tree
  traversal, and problems that naturally fit the divide-and-
  conquer paradigm.
- Use **iteration** for tasks like processing arrays or
  sequences where the solution can be expressed more
  efficiently with loops.

3.4 Function Overloading and Default Arguments

C++ allows you to define multiple functions with the same
name, but with different parameter types or numbers. This
feature is known as **function overloading**. Additionally, you
can provide default values for function parameters, making
them optional when calling the function.

3.4.1 Function Overloading

Function overloading allows you to create multiple versions
of a function that differ in the number or types of parameters.

- **Example of Function Overloading**:

```cpp
cpp

int add(int a, int b) {
    return a + b;
}

float add(float a, float b) {
    return a + b;
}

int add(int a, int b, int c) {
    return a + b + c;
}
```

In the above example, the `add` function is overloaded to handle different types of arguments and different numbers of parameters.

3.4.2 Default Arguments

Default arguments allow you to define default values for one or more function parameters. If the caller doesn't provide a value for the parameter, the default value is used.

- **Example of Default Arguments**:

```cpp
cpp
```

```cpp
void printMessage(std::string message =
"Hello, World!") {
    std::cout << message << std::endl;
}
```

In this case, if `printMessage()` is called without an argument, it will print "Hello, World!" by default.

- **Calling Functions with Default Arguments**:

cpp

```cpp
printMessage();   // Uses   the   default
argument
printMessage("Custom   message");   // Uses
the provided argument
```

- **Best Practice**: Provide default arguments from right to left (i.e., parameters with default values should be listed at the end).

Conclusion

In this chapter, we've covered essential control structures in C++ including conditionals and loops, efficient function writing techniques, recursion vs. iteration, and function overloading with default arguments. Mastering these concepts will help you write clean, efficient, and maintainable code while giving you the flexibility to approach problems in different ways.

CHAPTER 4

OBJECT-ORIENTED PROGRAMMING (OOP) IN C++

Object-Oriented Programming (OOP) is one of the cornerstones of modern C++ development. It provides a structure for organizing and managing code by grouping related data and functions into entities called **classes** and **objects**. This chapter covers the fundamental concepts of OOP, including classes and objects, constructors and destructors, inheritance, polymorphism, encapsulation, and operator overloading.

4.1 Classes and Objects

A **class** is a blueprint or template for creating objects, which are instances of that class. Classes define the properties (data members) and behaviors (member functions or methods) that objects of that class will have.

4.1.1 Defining a Class

A class is defined using the `class` keyword followed by the
class name and a set of curly braces containing the data
members and member functions.

cpp

```cpp
class Person {
public:
    // Data members
    std::string name;
    int age;

    // Member function
    void introduce() {
        std::cout << "Hello, my name is " << name
<< " and I am " << age << " years old." <<
std::endl;
    }
};
```

In this example:

- The `Person` class has two data members: `name` and `age`.
- The class has one member function, `introduce()`,
  which outputs a message introducing the person.

4.1.2 Creating Objects

Once a class is defined, you can create objects (instances of the class).

cpp

```
int main() {
    // Creating an object of the Person class
    Person p1;
    p1.name = "Alice";
    p1.age = 30;
    p1.introduce();  // Output: Hello, my name is
Alice and I am 30 years old.

    return 0;
}
```

Here, p1 is an object of the Person class, and we access its properties and methods using the dot (.) operator.

4.2 Constructors and Destructors

Constructors and **destructors** are special member functions in C++ that are used to initialize and clean up objects, respectively.

4.2.1 Constructors

A **constructor** is a special function that is automatically
called when an object of a class is created. Its purpose is to
initialize the object's data members.

- **Default Constructor**: A constructor with no
  parameters.

  cpp

  ```cpp
  class Person {
  public:
      std::string name;
      int age;

      // Default constructor
      Person() {
          name = "Unknown";
          age = 0;
      }
  };
  ```

- **Parameterized Constructor**: A constructor that
  takes parameters to initialize data members.

  cpp

```cpp
class Person {
public:
    std::string name;
    int age;

    // Parameterized constructor
    Person(std::string n, int a) {
        name = n;
        age = a;
    }
};
```

- **Constructor Overloading**: You can have multiple constructors with different parameters.

cpp

```cpp
class Person {
public:
    std::string name;
    int age;

    // Default constructor
    Person() : name("Unknown"), age(0) {}

    // Parameterized constructor
    Person(std::string n, int a) : name(n), age(a) {}
};
```

4.2.2 Destructors

A **destructor** is a special function that is automatically called when an object is destroyed, usually when it goes out of scope. The destructor is used to free any resources allocated to the object, such as memory or file handles.

- **Destructor Declaration**: A destructor has the same name as the class but is preceded by a tilde (~).

cpp

```cpp
class Person {
public:
    std::string name;
    int age;

    // Destructor
    ~Person() {
        std::cout << "Person " << name <<
" is being destroyed." << std::endl;
    }
};
```

The destructor is automatically called when the object p1 in the following example goes out of scope:

cpp

```
Person p1("Alice", 30);   // Destructor will be
called when p1 goes out of scope
```

4.3 Inheritance, Polymorphism, and Encapsulation

These three concepts are the pillars of Object-Oriented Programming.

4.3.1 Inheritance

Inheritance allows a new class (derived class) to inherit the properties and behaviors of an existing class (base class). This promotes code reuse and helps create a hierarchical relationship between classes.

- **Base Class**:

cpp

```cpp
class Animal {
public:
    std::string name;

    void speak() {
        std::cout << name << " makes a
sound." << std::endl;
    }
};
```

- **Derived Class**:

cpp

```cpp
class Dog : public Animal {
public:
    void speak() {
        std::cout << name << " barks." <<
std::endl;
    }
};
```

- **Creating and Using Derived Class**:

cpp

```cpp
int main() {
    Dog dog1;
    dog1.name = "Buddy";
    dog1.speak();  // Output: Buddy barks.

    return 0;
}
```

The `Dog` class inherits the `name` data member and the `speak()` function from the `Animal` class. The `Dog` class also has the ability to override the `speak()` method to provide a specific implementation.

4.3.2 Polymorphism

Polymorphism allows methods to have different behaviors based on the object calling them. It comes in two forms: **compile-time** (function overloading, operator overloading) and **run-time** (virtual functions).

- **Runtime Polymorphism** with Virtual Functions:

  By using **virtual functions**, C++ allows derived classes to override base class methods, enabling dynamic method binding at runtime.

  cpp

```cpp
class Animal {
public:
    virtual void speak() {
        std::cout << "Animal makes a sound." << std::endl;
    }
};

class Dog : public Animal {
public:
    void speak() override {
        std::cout << "Dog barks." << std::endl;
```

```cpp
    }
};

class Cat : public Animal {
public:
    void speak() override {
        std::cout << "Cat meows." << std::endl;
    }
};
```

o **Using Polymorphism**:

cpp

```cpp
int main() {
    Animal* animal1 = new Dog();
    animal1->speak();    // Output: Dog barks.

    Animal* animal2 = new Cat();
    animal2->speak();    // Output: Cat meows.

    delete animal1;
    delete animal2;

    return 0;
}
```

In this example, the `speak()` method is overridden in the Dog and Cat classes, and the correct method is called based on the type of object (polymorphism).

4.3.3 Encapsulation

Encapsulation is the practice of keeping fields (data members) and methods (functions) private to the class, exposing only necessary parts via public methods. This helps in hiding the internal implementation and protecting the data.

- **Private and Public Members**:

cpp

```cpp
class Person {
private:
    std::string name;   // Private member
    int age;            // Private member

public:
    // Public method to access private data
    void setName(std::string n) {
        name = n;
    }

    void setAge(int a) {
```

```
        age = a;
    }


    void introduce() {
        std::cout << "Name: " << name << ",
Age: " << age << std::endl;
    }
};
```

Encapsulation ensures that only specific functions can modify the internal data of the object, providing better control and security.

4.4 Operator Overloading

Operator overloading allows you to redefine the behavior of operators (like +, -, *, etc.) for user-defined types (classes).

4.4.1 Overloading Operators

You can overload operators to perform custom operations on objects. For example, overloading the + operator to add two Complex numbers.

cpp

```
class Complex {
```

```cpp
public:
    int real, imag;

    Complex(int r, int i) : real(r), imag(i) {}

    // Overloading the + operator
    Complex operator+(const Complex& other) {
        return Complex(real + other.real, imag +
other.imag);
    }
};

int main() {
    Complex c1(1, 2), c2(3, 4);
    Complex c3 = c1 + c2;   // Uses overloaded +
operator
    std::cout << "Result: " << c3.real << " + "
<< c3.imag << "i" << std::endl;
    return 0;
}
```

In this example, the + operator is overloaded to add two Complex objects by adding their real and imaginary parts separately.

Conclusion

In this chapter, we explored the core concepts of Object-Oriented Programming (OOP) in C++. We learned how to define and use classes and objects, work with constructors and destructors, implement inheritance, polymorphism, and encapsulation, and perform operator overloading. Mastering OOP principles allows you to write cleaner, more maintainable, and reusable code, laying a strong foundation for complex software development.

CHAPTER 5

ADVANCED OOP CONCEPTS

In this chapter, we will explore some of the more advanced concepts of Object-Oriented Programming (OOP) in C++, including **virtual functions**, **pure virtual functions**, **abstract classes**, **interfaces**, **multiple inheritance**, and **the diamond problem**. We'll also cover **design patterns**, which are reusable solutions to common problems in software design. These concepts will help you write more flexible, maintainable, and scalable object-oriented code.

5.1 Virtual Functions and Pure Virtual Functions

Virtual functions are a cornerstone of **polymorphism**, allowing you to override methods in derived classes to provide specialized behavior. This enables runtime polymorphism, where the correct method is called based on the actual object type, not the type of the pointer or reference.

5.1.1 Virtual Functions

A **virtual function** is a member function in the base class that you expect to be overridden in derived classes. When you call a virtual function using a pointer or reference to the base class, C++ will use the version of the function that corresponds to the actual object type (this is known as *dynamic dispatch*).

- **Example**:

cpp

```cpp
class Animal {
public:
    virtual void sound() {
        std::cout << "Animal makes a sound." << std::endl;
    }
};

class Dog : public Animal {
public:
    void sound() override {
        std::cout << "Dog barks." << std::endl;
    }
};

class Cat : public Animal {
public:
    void sound() override {
```

```cpp
        std::cout << "Cat meows." <<
std::endl;
    }
};

int main() {
    Animal* animal1 = new Dog();
    animal1->sound();    // Output: Dog
barks.

    Animal* animal2 = new Cat();
    animal2->sound();    // Output: Cat
meows.

    delete animal1;
    delete animal2;

    return 0;
}
```

In this example, the sound() function is declared as **virtual** in the Animal class. When the function is called using a pointer to Animal, it calls the sound() method of the actual object type, whether it's a Dog or a Cat.

5.1.2 Pure Virtual Functions

A **pure virtual function** is a function that must be overridden in any derived class. A class that contains a pure virtual function becomes an **abstract class**, meaning it cannot be instantiated directly.

- **Syntax**: A pure virtual function is declared by assigning = 0 to the function declaration.

cpp

```cpp
class Shape {
public:
    virtual void draw() = 0;   // Pure
virtual function
};
```

- **Derived class implementing the pure virtual function**:

cpp

```cpp
class Circle : public Shape {
public:
    void draw() override {
        std::cout << "Drawing a Circle" <<
std::endl;
```

```cpp
    }
};

class Square : public Shape {
public:
    void draw() override {
        std::cout << "Drawing a Square" <<
std::endl;
    }
};

int main() {
    Shape* shape1 = new Circle();
    shape1->draw();   // Output: Drawing a
Circle

    Shape* shape2 = new Square();
    shape2->draw();   // Output: Drawing a
Square

    delete shape1;
    delete shape2;

    return 0;
}
```

In this example, Shape is an abstract class with a pure virtual

function draw(). Both Circle and Square classes override

this function, and objects of those classes can be created and used.

5.2 Abstract Classes and Interfaces

An **abstract class** is a class that cannot be instantiated because it contains one or more pure virtual functions. **Interfaces** in C++ are typically implemented as abstract classes with only pure virtual functions and no data members or implementation.

5.2.1 Abstract Classes

An **abstract class** is used as a base class, and its derived classes must implement the pure virtual functions.

- **Example**:

cpp

```cpp
class AbstractClass {
public:
    virtual void display() = 0;   // Pure
virtual function
    void commonMethod() {
        std::cout << "Common    method
implementation" << std::endl;
    }
```

```
};
```

An abstract class can also have concrete (non-pure)
functions, as seen with `commonMethod()`. Derived classes
are still required to implement any pure virtual functions.

5.2.2 Interfaces

An interface is a class that only declares pure virtual
functions and has no implementation. In C++, interfaces are
typically represented using abstract classes.

- **Example**:

```cpp
cpp

class Drawable {
public:
    virtual void draw() = 0;    // Pure
virtual function
};

class Shape : public Drawable {
public:
    void draw() override {
        std::cout << "Shape is being
drawn." << std::endl;
    }
```

```
};
```

In this example, `Drawable` serves as an interface that any drawable object must implement. The `Shape` class implements the `draw()` function, making it a concrete class that can be instantiated.

5.3 Multiple Inheritance and the Diamond Problem

Multiple inheritance occurs when a class is derived from more than one base class. While powerful, it introduces potential complexities, such as the **diamond problem**, which occurs when a class inherits from two classes that have a common base class.

5.3.1 Multiple Inheritance

In C++, you can derive a class from more than one class, and it will inherit properties and methods from all of them.

- **Example**:

cpp

```cpp
class A {
public:
    void methodA() {
```

```cpp
        std::cout << "Method from A" <<
std::endl;
    }
};

class B {
public:
    void methodB() {
        std::cout << "Method from B" <<
std::endl;
    }
};

class C : public A, public B {
public:
    void methodC() {
        std::cout << "Method from C" <<
std::endl;
    }
};

int main() {
    C obj;
    obj.methodA();  // Output: Method from
A
    obj.methodB();  // Output: Method from
B
    obj.methodC();  // Output: Method from
C
```

```
    return 0;
}
```

5.3.2 The Diamond Problem

The **diamond problem** arises when a class inherits from two classes that both inherit from a common base class. This can create ambiguity if the derived class needs to access members of the common base class.

- **Example**:

cpp

```cpp
class A {
public:
    void methodA() {
        std::cout << "Method from A" <<
std::endl;
    }
};

class B : public A {
public:
    void methodB() {
        std::cout << "Method from B" <<
std::endl;
    }
```

```cpp
};

class C : public A {
public:
    void methodC() {
        std::cout << "Method from C" <<
std::endl;
    }
};

class D : public B, public C {
public:
    void methodD() {
        std::cout << "Method from D" <<
std::endl;
    }
};

int main() {
    D obj;
    obj.methodA();  // Ambiguous methodA()
call due to inheritance from both B and C
    obj.methodB();  // Output: Method from
B
    obj.methodC();  // Output: Method from
C
    obj.methodD();  // Output: Method from
D
```

71

```
        return 0;
}
```

In this example, class D inherits from both B and C, which each inherit from A. This leads to ambiguity when calling methodA() because both B and C have inherited it from A.

5.3.3 Solving the Diamond Problem

To solve the diamond problem, C++ uses **virtual inheritance**. This ensures that the common base class (A) is only included once in the derived class (D).

- **Example with Virtual Inheritance**:

cpp

```cpp
class A {
public:
    void methodA() {
        std::cout << "Method from A" << std::endl;
    }
};

class B : virtual public A {
public:
    void methodB() {
```

```cpp
        std::cout << "Method from B" <<
std::endl;
    }
};


class C : virtual public A {
public:
    void methodC() {
        std::cout << "Method from C" <<
std::endl;
    }
};


class D : public B, public C {
public:
    void methodD() {
        std::cout << "Method from D" <<
std::endl;
    }
};


int main() {
    D obj;
    obj.methodA();  // Output: Method from
A
    obj.methodB();  // Output: Method from
B
    obj.methodC();  // Output: Method from
C
```

```
    obj.methodD();   // Output: Method from
D

    return 0;
}
```

By using `virtual` inheritance, class D will only have a single instance of class A, solving the ambiguity.

5.4 Design Patterns in C++

Design patterns are proven solutions to recurring software design problems. They help make your code more flexible, reusable, and easier to maintain.

5.4.1 Types of Design Patterns

- **Creational Patterns**: Deal with object creation mechanisms, trying to create objects in a manner suitable to the situation. Example: **Singleton, Factory**.
- **Structural Patterns**: Concerned with how classes and objects are composed to form larger structures. Example: **Adapter, Decorator**.
- **Behavioral Patterns**: Deal with object interaction and responsibilities. Example: **Observer, Strategy**.

5.4.2 Example: Singleton Pattern

The **Singleton** pattern ensures a class has only one instance and provides a global access point to that instance.

- **Singleton Implementation**:

cpp

```cpp
class Singleton {
private:
    static Singleton* instance;
    Singleton() {}  // Private constructor

public:
    static Singleton* getInstance() {
        if (instance == nullptr) {
            instance = new Singleton();
        }
        return instance;
    }
};

Singleton* Singleton::instance = nullptr;

int main() {
    Singleton*         s1         =
Singleton::getInstance();
```

```
        Singleton*                s2              =
Singleton::getInstance();
        // s1 and s2 will point to the same
instance
        return 0;
}
```

In this example, the `Singleton` class ensures that only one
instance is created and provides access through
`getInstance()`.

Conclusion

This chapter covered some of the more advanced OOP
concepts in C++, including virtual functions, pure virtual
functions, abstract classes, interfaces, multiple inheritance,
and design patterns. These concepts are fundamental for
writing flexible, maintainable, and reusable code.
Understanding and mastering these advanced OOP features
will enable you to design robust software systems that scale
efficiently and manage complex relationships between
objects.

CHAPTER 6

TEMPLATES AND GENERIC PROGRAMMING

C++ templates are a powerful feature that allows you to write flexible, reusable, and efficient code. Templates enable generic programming, where functions and classes can work with any data type. This chapter will introduce you to function and class templates, explore template specialization, advanced techniques like SFINAE and variadic templates, and provide real-world examples of how templates are used in C++.

6.1 Introduction to Templates (Function and Class Templates)

Templates in C++ are a mechanism for writing code that works with any data type. A template can be used to create functions or classes that are independent of the data types they operate on, enabling code reuse and flexibility.

6.1.1 Function Templates

A **function template** allows you to define a function that works with any data type. Instead of defining a separate function for each data type, you can write one function that works for any type.

- **Example**: A template function for swapping two values of any type:

cpp

```cpp
#include <iostream>
using namespace std;

template <typename T>
void swapValues(T& a, T& b) {
    T temp = a;
    a = b;
    b = temp;
}

int main() {
    int x = 10, y = 20;
    swapValues(x, y);
    cout << "x = " << x << ", y = " << y << endl;
// Output: x = 20, y = 10
```

```cpp
    double a = 3.14, b = 1.59;
    swapValues(a, b);
    cout << "a = " << a << ", b = " << b << endl;
// Output: a = 1.59, b = 3.14

    return 0;
}
```

In this example, the `swapValues` function is a template that works for any type `T`. The type `T` is determined at compile time when the function is called.

- **Template Parameter**: The `typename` `T` in the `swapValues` function indicates that `T` is a placeholder for the data type.

6.1.2 Class Templates

A **class template** allows you to define a class that can work with any data type, similar to function templates. This provides a way to create generic data structures, such as linked lists, stacks, and queues.

- **Example**: A class template for a simple generic container:

cpp

```cpp
#include <iostream>
```

```cpp
using namespace std;

template <typename T>
class Box {
private:
    T value;

public:
    void setValue(T v) { value = v; }
    T getValue() { return value; }
};

int main() {
    Box<int> intBox;
    intBox.setValue(10);
    cout    <<      "Integer     value:      "    <<
intBox.getValue() << endl;

    Box<double> doubleBox;
    doubleBox.setValue(3.14);
    cout    <<      "Double      value:      "    <<
doubleBox.getValue() << endl;

    return 0;
}
```

In this example, the Box class is a template that can hold any
type of value. The class is instantiated with different types

(e.g., `Box<int>` and `Box<double>`) to create objects that store `int` and `double` values, respectively.

6.2 Template Specialization

Template specialization allows you to define a specific implementation of a template for a particular data type. This is useful when you need a different behavior for a specific type, while still maintaining the general functionality for other types.

6.2.1 Full Specialization

Full specialization occurs when you define a completely different implementation for a specific type.

- **Example**: Specializing the `Box` class template for `char` type:

cpp

```
#include <iostream>
using namespace std;

template <typename T>
class Box {
public:
```

```cpp
    T value;
    void setValue(T v) { value = v; }
    T getValue() { return value; }
};


// Specialization for char type
template <>
class Box<char> {
public:
    char value;
    void setValue(char v) { value = v; }
    char getValue() { return value; }
    void printChar() { cout << "Character value:
" << value << endl; }
};


int main() {
    Box<int> intBox;
    intBox.setValue(10);
    cout << "Integer value: " <<
intBox.getValue() << endl;


    Box<char> charBox;
    charBox.setValue('A');
    cout << "Character value: " <<
charBox.getValue() << endl;
    charBox.printChar();   // Output: Character
value: A
```

```
    return 0;
}
```

In this example, the `Box` template is specialized for the `char` type, where we add a specific method (`printChar()`) for `char` values.

6.2.2 Partial Specialization

Partial specialization allows you to specify a template for a specific subset of types, while keeping the rest of the template generic.

- **Example**: Specializing `Box` for pointer types:

cpp

```cpp
template <typename T>
class Box {
public:
    T value;
    void setValue(T v) { value = v; }
    T getValue() { return value; }
};

// Partial specialization for pointer types
template <typename T>
class Box<T*> {
```

```cpp
public:
    T* value;
    void setValue(T* v) { value = v; }
    T* getValue() { return value; }
    void printPointer() { cout << "Pointer value:
" << *value << endl; }
};

int main() {
    int num = 5;
    Box<int*> ptrBox;
    ptrBox.setValue(&num);
    cout << "Pointer    value:    " <<
*ptrBox.getValue() << endl;   // Output: Pointer
value: 5
    ptrBox.printPointer();   // Output: Pointer
value: 5

    return 0;
}
```

In this example, we partially specialize the Box class
template to work specifically with pointer types (T*).

6.3 Advanced Template Techniques

6.3.1 SFINAE (Substitution Failure Is Not An Error)

SFINAE is a technique that allows you to enable or disable template functions based on the properties of the template type. This is achieved using `std::enable_if` or type traits to selectively include or exclude certain functions from the compilation process.

- **Example**: Using `std::enable_if` to restrict a function to integer types:

cpp

```
#include <iostream>
#include <type_traits>
using namespace std;

// SFINAE example: Only accepts integer types
template <typename T>
typename
std::enable_if<std::is_integral<T>::value>::typ
e
printType(T value) {
    cout << "Integer value: " << value << endl;
}

int main() {
```

85

```cpp
    printType(10);   // Output: Integer value: 10
    // printType(3.14); // Compilation error: not
an integral type
    return 0;
}
```

In this example, the function `printType` only accepts integral types (like `int`, `long`, etc.). If you attempt to call it with a non-integral type, the function is excluded from the compilation via SFINAE.

6.3.2 Variadic Templates

Variadic templates allow you to create templates that accept a variable number of arguments. This is useful when you don't know in advance how many arguments will be passed to a function or class.

- **Example**: A variadic template function that prints any number of arguments:

cpp

```cpp
#include <iostream>
using namespace std;

template <typename... Args>
void printArgs(Args... args) {
```

```cpp
    (cout << ... << args) << endl;
}

int main() {
    printArgs(1, 2, 3, "Hello", 5.6);  // Output:
123Hello5.6
    return 0;
}
```

In this example, the `printArgs` function uses a variadic template to accept any number of arguments and print them all.

6.4 Real-World Use Cases of Templates

Templates are widely used in real-world applications due to their flexibility and efficiency. Below are a few examples of how templates are used in practical scenarios:

6.4.1 Standard Template Library (STL)

The **Standard Template Library (STL)** in C++ makes extensive use of templates. It includes generic algorithms, containers, and iterators that can work with any data type.

- **Example**: Using the `std::vector` container (a template class) to store and manipulate data:

cpp

```cpp
#include <vector>
#include <iostream>
using namespace std;

int main() {
    vector<int> numbers = {1, 2, 3, 4, 5};
    for (int num : numbers) {
        cout << num << " ";
    }
    cout << endl;   // Output: 1 2 3 4 5
    return 0;
}
```

In this example, the `std::vector<int>` is a template class that allows you to store integers in a dynamic array.

6.4.2 Type-Specific Algorithms

Templates are also used in implementing algorithms that work with different data types, such as sorting, searching, or data manipulation.

- **Example**: A template function that sorts an array:

cpp

```cpp
template <typename T>
void sortArray(T arr[], int size) {
    for (int i = 0; i < size - 1; ++i) {
        for (int j = i + 1; j < size; ++j) {
            if (arr[i] > arr[j]) {
                T temp = arr[i];
                arr[i] = arr[j];
                arr[j] = temp;
            }
        }
    }
}

int main() {
    int arr[] = {5, 2, 9, 1, 5, 6};
    int size = sizeof(arr) / sizeof(arr[0]);
    sortArray(arr, size);
    for (int num : arr) {
        cout << num << " ";   // Output: 1 2 5 5
6 9
    }
    return 0;
}
```

This template allows you to sort an array of any type, whether integers, floats, or custom data types.

Conclusion

In this chapter, we have learned about templates and how they enable **generic programming** in C++. We covered the basics of function and class templates, template specialization, and advanced techniques like SFINAE and variadic templates. We also explored real-world use cases of templates, such as their use in the Standard Template Library (STL) and custom algorithms. Mastering templates will help you write more flexible, efficient, and reusable code in C++.

CHAPTER 7

STANDARD TEMPLATE LIBRARY (STL)

The **Standard Template Library (STL)** is a powerful library in C++ that provides a collection of generic classes and functions for handling data structures and algorithms. It simplifies and standardizes common operations like data storage, iteration, and manipulation. In this chapter, we'll explore the core components of STL: containers, iterators, algorithms, design principles, and how to customize STL for user-defined types.

7.1 Introduction to STL Containers

Containers are objects that store collections of data. STL provides a variety of container classes that are designed to handle data in different ways, such as vectors, lists, maps, and sets. These containers are generic, meaning they can hold any data type.

7.1.1 Vectors

std::vector is one of the most commonly used containers in C++. It is a dynamic array that can grow or shrink in size as needed, making it more flexible than traditional arrays.

- **Example**: Using std::vector to store integers:

cpp

```cpp
#include <iostream>
#include <vector>
using namespace std;

int main() {
    vector<int> v = {10, 20, 30, 40, 50};
    v.push_back(60); // Adds an element to the
end of the vector

    for (int num : v) {
        cout << num << " ";  // Output: 10 20 30
40 50 60
    }
    cout << endl;

    v.pop_back(); // Removes the last element
    cout << "After pop_back: ";
    for (int num : v) {
```

```cpp
        cout << num << " ";   // Output: 10 20 30
40 50
    }
    cout << endl;

    return 0;
}
```

- **Features**:
  - o Dynamic resizing: `std::vector` automatically resizes as elements are added.
  - o Direct access to elements via indices.

7.1.2 Lists

`std::list` is a doubly-linked list that allows efficient insertion and removal of elements from both ends. Unlike `std::vector`, `std::list` provides no direct access to elements by index.

- **Example**: Using `std::list`:

cpp

```cpp
#include <iostream>
#include <list>
using namespace std;
```

```cpp
int main() {
    list<int> l = {10, 20, 30, 40};
    l.push_back(50);   // Adds an element to the
end
    l.push_front(5);   // Adds an element to the
front

    for (int num : l) {
        cout << num << " ";   // Output: 5 10 20
30 40 50
    }
    cout << endl;

    l.pop_back();   // Removes the last element
    l.pop_front(); // Removes the first element
    cout << "After pop operations: ";
    for (int num : l) {
        cout << num << " ";   // Output: 10 20 30
40
    }
    cout << endl;

    return 0;
}
```

- **Features**:
    o Efficient insertion and deletion at both ends.
    o No random access, meaning iterating through elements is done sequentially.

7.1.3 Maps

std::map is an associative container that stores key-value
pairs in a sorted order. The keys are unique, and each key
maps to exactly one value.

- **Example**: Using std::map:

cpp

```cpp
#include <iostream>
#include <map>
using namespace std;

int main() {
    map<string, int> age;
    age["Alice"] = 30;
    age["Bob"] = 25;
    age["Charlie"] = 35;

    for (const auto& pair : age) {
        cout << pair.first << ": " << pair.second
<< endl;  // Output: Alice: 30, Bob: 25, Charlie:
35
    }

    return 0;
}
```

- **Features**:
  - ○ Stores key-value pairs, sorted by keys.
  - ○ Fast lookup, insertion, and deletion of key-value pairs.

7.1.4 Sets

`std::set` is an associative container that stores unique elements in a sorted order. It does not store duplicates, and it automatically keeps its elements sorted.

- **Example**: Using `std::set`:

cpp

```cpp
#include <iostream>
#include <set>
using namespace std;

int main() {
    set<int> s = {10, 20, 30, 40, 50};
    s.insert(60);   // Adds an element to the set

    for (int num : s) {
        cout << num << " ";   // Output: 10 20 30
40 50 60
    }
    cout << endl;
```

```
    s.erase(30);    // Removes the element with
value 30
    cout << "After erase: ";
    for (int num : s) {
        cout << num << " ";   // Output: 10 20 40
50 60
    }
    cout << endl;

    return 0;
}
```

- **Features**:
  - o Stores unique elements, sorted automatically.
  - o Fast lookup, insertion, and deletion.

7.2 Iterators and Algorithms in STL

Iterators are objects that allow you to traverse through the elements of a container, and they are an essential part of the STL. STL also provides a wide range of algorithms that can be used to perform operations on containers, such as searching, sorting, and modifying elements.

7.2.1 Iterators

An **iterator** is an object that points to an element within a container. It provides a way to access container elements sequentially without exposing the underlying structure of the container.

- **Example**: Using iterators with `std::vector`:

cpp

```cpp
#include <iostream>
#include <vector>
using namespace std;

int main() {
    vector<int> v = {10, 20, 30, 40, 50};

    // Using an iterator to traverse the vector
    for (vector<int>::iterator it = v.begin(); it != v.end(); ++it) {
        cout << *it << " ";   // Output: 10 20 30 40 50
    }
    cout << endl;

    return 0;
}
```

- **Common iterator operations**:
  - `begin()`: Returns an iterator pointing to the first element.
  - `end()`: Returns an iterator pointing past the last element (one position beyond the last element).
  - `++it`: Increments the iterator to point to the next element.
  - `*it`: Dereferences the iterator to access the value.

7.2.2 Algorithms

The STL provides a variety of algorithms that can be used with containers. These algorithms include operations for searching, sorting, modifying, and combining elements.

- **Example**: Using `std::sort` and `std::find`:

cpp

```cpp
#include <iostream>
#include <vector>
#include <algorithm>  // For sort and find
using namespace std;

int main() {
    vector<int> v = {40, 10, 30, 20, 50};

    // Sorting the vector
```

99

```cpp
    sort(v.begin(), v.end());      // Sort in
ascending order
    for (int num : v) {
        cout << num << " ";  // Output: 10 20 30
40 50
    }
    cout << endl;

    // Finding an element
    auto it = find(v.begin(), v.end(), 30);   //
Find element 30
    if (it != v.end()) {
        cout << "Found: " << *it << endl;   //
Output: Found: 30
    }

    return 0;
}
```

- **Common STL algorithms**:
    o   sort(): Sorts elements in a container.
    o   find(): Searches for an element in a container.
    o   reverse(): Reverses the order of elements.
    o   accumulate(): Sums the elements of a container.
    o   for_each(): Applies a function to each element.

7.3 STL Design Principles and Usage

The design of the STL is based on a few key principles that make it flexible, efficient, and easy to use:

- **Generic Programming**: The STL is designed to work with any data type, allowing containers, iterators, and algorithms to be used with any user-defined or built-in types.

- **Separation of Concerns**: Containers, iterators, and algorithms are designed as separate entities. This allows you to mix and match containers with different algorithms and iterators.

- **Efficiency**: STL containers and algorithms are optimized for performance. They make use of efficient data structures and algorithms, minimizing overhead.

7.3.1 Common Usage Patterns

- **Container and Algorithm Pairing**: The STL allows you to choose the best container for your data and then apply the most appropriate algorithm. For example, you might use `std::vector` with `std::sort`, or `std::map` with `std::find`.

- **Iterators as Abstractions**: Iterators abstract away the details of the container's internal structure. Whether you are working with a `std::vector`, `std::list`, or std::map, you can use the same iterators to access and modify the elements.

7.4 Customizing STL with User-Defined Types

The STL is designed to work with custom user-defined types. By providing the appropriate operator overloads and comparisons, you can use STL containers and algorithms with your own data types.

7.4.1 Overloading Comparison Operators

To use your custom data types with STL containers like std::set or std::map, you must overload comparison operators like <, >, or ==.

- **Example**: Using a custom Person class with std::set:

cpp

```
#include <iostream>
#include <set>
using namespace std;

class Person {
public:
    string name;
    int age;
```

```cpp
    Person(string n, int a) : name(n), age(a) {}

    bool operator<(const Person& other) const {
        return age < other.age;   // Compare by
age
    }
};

int main() {
    set<Person> people;
    people.insert(Person("Alice", 30));
    people.insert(Person("Bob", 25));
    people.insert(Person("Charlie", 35));

    for (const Person& p : people) {
        cout << p.name << ": " << p.age << endl;
// Output sorted by age
    }

    return 0;
}
```

- **Explanation**:
    - o We overloaded the < operator to define how Person objects should be compared.

o This allows us to use the `Person` class in STL
containers like `std::set`, which relies on
comparisons for ordering.

Conclusion

In this chapter, we've covered the essentials of the **Standard
Template Library (STL),** including containers, iterators,
algorithms, and how to customize STL with user-defined
types. STL provides a rich set of tools for handling
collections of data and applying common operations
efficiently. By understanding how to use STL containers and
algorithms, as well as how to customize them for your types,
you can significantly improve the flexibility,
maintainability, and performance of your C++ programs.

CHAPTER 8

MULTITHREADING AND CONCURRENCY IN C++

Multithreading and concurrency are essential concepts for modern software development. By leveraging multiple threads of execution, we can improve the performance and responsiveness of applications, especially when dealing with CPU-bound tasks or I/O operations. In this chapter, we will explore how to manage threads and synchronize their execution in C++, covering key concepts such as mutexes, locks, condition variables, and thread pooling.

8.1 Introduction to Multithreading

Multithreading is the concept of executing multiple threads concurrently within a program. A **thread** is the smallest unit of a CPU's execution, and multithreading allows multiple threads to execute different parts of a program at the same time, making efficient use of multi-core processors.

8.1.1 Benefits of Multithreading

- **Improved Performance**: By running tasks in parallel on different CPU cores, multithreading can improve the performance of CPU-bound tasks.
- **Responsiveness**: Multithreading allows programs to remain responsive, especially in applications with heavy I/O operations (e.g., GUI applications or server-side programs).
- **Better Resource Utilization**: Modern processors have multiple cores. Multithreading ensures that your program can utilize these cores effectively.

8.1.2 Threading in C++

C++11 introduced a standardized threading library that provides basic tools for creating and managing threads. The key components for working with threads in C++ are found in the `<thread>` header.

- **Creating a Thread**: A thread is created by passing a function to the `std::thread` constructor.

cpp

```cpp
#include <iostream>
#include <thread>
```

```cpp
using namespace std;

void hello() {
    cout << "Hello from thread!" << endl;
}

int main() {
    thread t(hello);    // Start a new thread
running the function hello()
    t.join();  // Wait for the thread to finish
    return 0;
}
```

- **join()**: The join() function blocks the calling thread until the thread t has finished executing.
- **detach()**: The detach() function allows the thread to run independently of the main thread, but without being able to join it.

8.2 Thread Management and Synchronization

Managing threads involves starting, controlling, and terminating threads safely. Synchronization is necessary to avoid issues that arise when multiple threads access shared resources simultaneously.

8.2.1 Race Conditions and Data Consistency

A **race condition** occurs when two or more threads access shared data simultaneously, and at least one thread modifies the data. This can lead to inconsistent or corrupted data. To prevent race conditions, synchronization mechanisms are used.

8.2.2 Synchronization Mechanisms

Synchronization ensures that only one thread accesses a critical section of code (shared data or resource) at a time, preventing race conditions and ensuring data consistency.

- **Mutexes (Mutual Exclusion)**: A **mutex** is a synchronization primitive used to protect shared data. It prevents multiple threads from accessing the same resource concurrently.

cpp

```
#include <iostream>
#include <thread>
#include <mutex>
using namespace std;

mutex mtx;
```

```cpp
void printNumber(int num) {
    mtx.lock();  // Lock the mutex
    cout << "Number: " << num << endl;
    mtx.unlock();  // Unlock the mutex
}

int main() {
    thread t1(printNumber, 1);
    thread t2(printNumber, 2);

    t1.join();
    t2.join();

    return 0;
}
```

- **std::mutex**: Provides the `lock()` and `unlock()` methods for manual lock management. It's important to always unlock a mutex after it has been locked to avoid deadlock situations.

8.2.3 Scoped Locking and `std::lock_guard`

Using `lock()` and `unlock()` manually can be error-prone. To simplify this, C++ provides **std::lock_guard**, which automatically locks and unlocks a mutex.

cpp

```cpp
#include <iostream>
#include <thread>
#include <mutex>
using namespace std;

mutex mtx;

void printNumber(int num) {
    lock_guard<mutex>    guard(mtx);    // Automatically locks and unlocks the mutex
    cout << "Number: " << num << endl;
}

int main() {
    thread t1(printNumber, 1);
    thread t2(printNumber, 2);

    t1.join();
    t2.join();

    return 0;
}
```

- **std::lock_guard** ensures that the mutex is locked at the beginning of the scope and unlocked at the end, even if an exception occurs.

8.2.4 Condition Variables

Condition variables are used for thread synchronization when threads need to wait for certain conditions to be met before continuing execution. A **condition variable** allows threads to block until a particular condition is true.

- **Example**: Using a condition variable to synchronize threads:

cpp

```cpp
#include <iostream>
#include <thread>
#include <mutex>
#include <condition_variable>
using namespace std;

mutex mtx;
condition_variable cv;
bool ready = false;

void printNumber(int num) {
    unique_lock<mutex> lock(mtx);   // Lock mutex
with unique_lock

    while (!ready) {
```

```cpp
        cv.wait(lock);   // Wait until 'ready' is
true
    }
    cout << "Number: " << num << endl;
}

void setReady() {
    this_thread::sleep_for(chrono::seconds(1));
    {
        lock_guard<mutex> lock(mtx);
        ready = true;  // Set ready to true after
1 second
    }
    cv.notify_all();      // Notify  all  waiting
threads
}

int main() {
    thread t1(printNumber, 1);
    thread t2(printNumber, 2);
    thread t3(setReady);

    t1.join();
    t2.join();
    t3.join();

    return 0;
}
```

- **wait()**: The `wait()` function causes the calling thread to block until the condition variable is notified.
- **notify_all()**: This function wakes up all threads that are waiting on the condition variable.

8.3 Mutexes, Locks, and Condition Variables

- **std::mutex**: A mutual exclusion lock that ensures only one thread can access a shared resource at a time.
- **std::lock_guard**: A simple, exception-safe way to manage locking/unlocking of mutexes.
- **std::unique_lock**: A more flexible lock management tool, offering more control than `lock_guard` (e.g., can be locked and unlocked manually).
- **std::condition_variable**: A synchronization tool used for thread coordination, allowing threads to wait until certain conditions are true.

These tools are vital for writing thread-safe programs and ensuring data consistency when multiple threads access shared resources.

8.4 Practical Examples: Thread Pooling and Task Parallelism

8.4.1 Thread Pooling

A **thread pool** is a collection of worker threads that are used to execute multiple tasks concurrently. Thread pools are useful when you need to repeatedly perform tasks in parallel but do not want to create and destroy threads each time a task is executed. Instead, threads are reused.

- **Example**: Simple thread pool implementation using `std::thread`:

cpp

```cpp
#include <iostream>
#include <thread>
#include <vector>
#include <functional>
using namespace std;

class ThreadPool {
private:
    vector<thread> workers;

public:
    // Constructor to create a pool of threads
    ThreadPool(int numThreads) {
        for (int i = 0; i < numThreads; ++i) {
```

```cpp
workers.push_back(thread(&ThreadPool::workerFunction, this));
        }
    }

    // Worker thread function
    void workerFunction() {
        while (true) {
            cout << "Worker thread is working..." << endl;

this_thread::sleep_for(chrono::seconds(1));    // Simulate work
        }
    }

    // Destructor to join all threads (clean up)
    ~ThreadPool() {
        for (auto& worker : workers) {
            worker.join();
        }
    }
};

int main() {
    ThreadPool pool(3);  // Create a thread pool with 3 threads
```

```
    this_thread::sleep_for(chrono::seconds(5));
// Let threads run for 5 seconds

    return 0;
}
```

In this simple thread pool example, we create a pool of threads that continuously execute a worker function. In a real-world application, you would add task queues and manage the execution of different tasks, but this basic example shows how to create and manage a thread pool.

8.4.2 Task Parallelism

Task parallelism refers to breaking a program into smaller tasks that can be executed in parallel. Each task runs independently, and the results are combined at the end.

- **Example**: Using `std::async` and `std::future` for task parallelism:

cpp

```
#include <iostream>
#include <future>
using namespace std;

int computeSum(int a, int b) {
```

```cpp
    return a + b;
}


int main() {
    // Launch a task asynchronously
    future<int> result = async(launch::async,
computeSum, 5, 10);

    // Do some other work
    cout << "Doing some other work..." << endl;

    // Get the result from the asynchronous task
    cout << "The sum is: " << result.get() <<
endl;  // Output: The sum is: 15

    return 0;
}
```

- **std::async**: Launches a task asynchronously and returns a std::future object, which can be used to get the result of the computation.
- **std::future::get()**: Blocks until the result is available and retrieves the result of the asynchronous task.

Conclusion

In this chapter, we explored the basics of **multithreading** and **concurrency** in C++. We learned about thread creation

117

and management, thread synchronization using **mutexes, locks**, and **condition variables**, and how to solve common concurrency problems. We also looked at practical examples such as **thread pooling** and **task parallelism**, which are powerful tools for creating efficient and responsive multi-threaded applications. By mastering these concepts, you will be able to write programs that make full use of modern multi-core processors, enhancing both performance and responsiveness.

CHAPTER 9

MEMORY OPTIMIZATION AND PERFORMANCE TUNING

In modern software development, optimizing memory usage and improving performance are key to creating efficient applications. Whether you are building resource-intensive systems or applications with large datasets, focusing on **time complexity**, **space complexity**, and **runtime overhead** can make a significant difference in the efficiency of your code. This chapter covers strategies for optimizing memory and performance in C++, from profiling tools to caching techniques.

9.1 Optimizing for Time and Space Complexity

Optimizing time and space complexity involves improving how your code executes (time) and how it uses memory (space). By reducing the resources required for running an algorithm, you can significantly enhance the performance of your application.

119

9.1.1 Time Complexity Optimization

Time complexity refers to the amount of time an algorithm takes to run relative to its input size. In C++, optimizing for time complexity typically involves selecting more efficient algorithms and data structures.

- **Use of Efficient Algorithms**: Choose algorithms with lower time complexity (e.g., O(n log n) instead of O(n^2)).
    - o Example: Replacing a bubble sort algorithm (O(n^2)) with quicksort (O(n log n)) can drastically improve performance for larger datasets.
- **Use of Faster Data Structures**: Some data structures provide faster access and modification times for specific operations.
    - o Example: Using `std::unordered_map` (which has average O(1) lookup time) instead of `std::map` (which has O(log n) lookup time) when you don't need elements to be ordered.
- **Loop Optimization**: Loop operations are often the most time-consuming part of a program. To optimize loops:
    - o Minimize redundant calculations inside the loop.

o Use `reserve()` to avoid repeated resizing of
dynamic arrays like `std::vector`.

cpp

```
std::vector<int> vec;
vec.reserve(1000); // Reserve memory in
advance to avoid resizing during insertions
for (int i = 0; i < 1000; ++i) {
    vec.push_back(i);
}
```

9.1.2 Space Complexity Optimization

Space complexity refers to the amount of memory an
algorithm uses relative to its input size. Optimizing space
complexity involves reducing the amount of memory
required for your data structures.

- **In-place Algorithms**: Whenever possible, modify
  data in place rather than using additional memory.
    o Example: Sorting a list in-place instead of
      creating a new sorted list reduces space usage.
- **Data Structure Choice**: Some data structures
  consume more memory than others. Consider using
  more memory-efficient structures for your use case.

o Example: A `std::vector` may be more space-efficient than a `std::list` for random access operations, while `std::list` may be more space-efficient than `std::vector` for frequent insertions and deletions.

- **Reducing Memory Footprint**: Eliminate unnecessary data copies. Pass data by reference or use pointers when ing large objects or arrays.

9.1.3 Time and Space Complexity Trade-offs

In some cases, optimizing for time may increase space complexity, or vice versa. Balancing these trade-offs is crucial, depending on the application's specific needs:

- **Example**: A hash table may provide fast lookups (O(1)) but consume more memory compared to a balanced binary search tree (O(log n)).

9.2 Profiling Tools and Techniques

Profiling helps you identify performance bottlenecks in your application, allowing you to focus your optimization efforts on the areas that will have the greatest impact. C++ provides several tools and techniques for profiling code.

9.2.1 Profiling Techniques

- **Manual Timing**: You can manually time sections of your code to identify where most time is spent. The <chrono> library provides high-precision timers.

cpp

```cpp
#include <iostream>
#include <chrono>
using namespace std;
using namespace chrono;

int main() {
    auto                start             =
high_resolution_clock::now();

    // Code block to profile
    for (int i = 0; i < 1000000; ++i) {
        int x = i * i;
    }

    auto                end               =
high_resolution_clock::now();
    auto                duration          =
duration_cast<microseconds>(end - start);
```

```
    cout      <<      "Duration:     "    <<
    duration.count()  <<  "  microseconds"  <<
    endl;

    return 0;
}
```

- **Built-in Profilers**: Tools such as `gprof` and `perf` (on Linux) allow you to profile your application more comprehensively.

  o **gprof**: Collects information about the time spent in each function of the program.

  o **perf**: Provides performance counter information, such as CPU cycles, cache misses, etc.

- **Memory Profiling**: Tools like **Valgrind** and **AddressSanitizer** help detect memory leaks, memory access errors, and memory usage bottlenecks.

  o **Valgrind**: Tracks memory allocations and deallocations, helping to find memory leaks.

  o **AddressSanitizer**: Detects memory corruption and undefined memory accesses.

9.2.2 Profiling Libraries

- **Google Performance Tools (gperftools)**: Provides libraries for heap profiling, CPU profiling, and thread profiling.
- **Intel VTune Profiler**: A more advanced profiling tool that provides deep insights into performance and optimization opportunities.

9.3 Caching and Memory Access Patterns

Efficient memory access patterns and caching strategies are crucial for improving performance. **Cache locality** refers to the concept of accessing memory in a way that optimizes the CPU cache. By ensuring data is used efficiently, we can minimize costly cache misses.

9.3.1 Caching Strategies

- **Data Locality**: Accessing contiguous memory blocks increases the likelihood of cache hits. This is particularly relevant for arrays or vectors.
  - **Example**: Using `std::vector` to store a large dataset instead of a `std::list` increases the chances of cache locality because vectors store data in contiguous memory.

- **Blocking (or Tiling)**: For certain large-scale computations (e.g., matrix multiplication), dividing the problem into smaller chunks that fit into cache can significantly improve performance.
    - o **Example**: In matrix multiplication, using small sub-matrices (blocks) that fit in the cache can reduce cache misses.

9.3.2 Optimizing Cache Usage

- **Access Patterns**: Try to access memory in a sequential or predictable pattern. This helps maximize cache hits and reduce cache misses.
    - o **Example**: In a loop that processes a 2D matrix, access the elements row-by-row (if the matrix is stored in row-major order), as this improves cache locality.

cpp

```cpp
// Good cache access pattern (row-major order)
for (int i = 0; i < rows; ++i) {
    for (int j = 0; j < cols; ++j) {
        // Access matrix[i][j]
    }
}
```

- **Pre-fetching**: Manually prefetching data into the cache before it is accessed can sometimes improve performance. Many modern compilers provide automatic prefetching, but in certain cases, explicit prefetching using compiler-specific hints can help.

9.3.3 Optimizing Memory Access Patterns

- **Strided Access**: Accessing data at a stride (e.g., every nth element) can cause cache misses if the stride is large, as it bypasses the cache. Try to minimize strided access when possible.
- **Alignment**: Ensure that data is aligned properly in memory to optimize cache access. For example, use **alignas** or memory allocators that provide aligned memory.

cpp

```
alignas(64) int arr[1000];   // Ensures that arr
is aligned to 64-byte boundaries
```

9.4 Minimizing Runtime Overhead

Minimizing runtime overhead involves optimizing code to reduce unnecessary computations, memory allocations, and other operations that slow down the program.

9.4.1 Inlining Functions

Inlining small functions can reduce the overhead of function calls, especially in tight loops. In C++, the `inline` keyword suggests that the compiler replaces the function call with the function's code.

cpp

```cpp
inline int add(int a, int b) {
    return a + b;
}
```

However, note that overusing `inline` can increase code size and reduce cache efficiency, so it should be used judiciously.

9.4.2 Loop Unrolling

Loop unrolling is an optimization technique where the body of a loop is expanded to reduce the overhead of looping. This can improve performance by reducing the number of iterations and the associated branching.

cpp

```cpp
// Before unrolling
for (int i = 0; i < n; ++i) {
```

```
    arr[i] = i;
}


// After unrolling
for (int i = 0; i < n; i += 4) {
    arr[i] = i;
    arr[i+1] = i+1;
    arr[i+2] = i+2;
    arr[i+3] = i+3;
}
```

9.4.3 Compiler Optimizations

Modern compilers offer various optimization flags that can improve runtime performance:

- **Optimization Levels**: Use flags like -O2 or -O3 in GCC or Clang to enable compiler optimizations.
- **Profile-Guided Optimization (PGO)**: This technique involves profiling the application and then using the profiling data to guide the compiler's optimizations.

Conclusion

In this chapter, we covered essential strategies for **memory optimization** and **performance tuning** in C++. We explored how to improve both **time** and **space complexity** by selecting efficient algorithms and data structures.

Profiling tools and techniques, such as using `gprof`, `perf`, and Valgrind, help identify bottlenecks and memory inefficiencies. We also learned about **caching strategies**, **memory access patterns**, and techniques to **minimize runtime overhead**, such as function inlining and loop unrolling. By applying these principles and using the appropriate tools, you can significantly improve the performance of your C++ applications.

CHAPTER 10

ADVANCED C++ FEATURES FOR HIGH-PERFORMANCE

C++ provides several advanced features that enhance both performance and flexibility in high-performance applications. In this chapter, we will explore some of these features, including **move semantics** and **r-value references**, **smart pointers**, **lambda functions**, **function objects**, and **type traits** and **metaprogramming**. These features enable developers to write more efficient, maintainable, and modern C++ code.

10.1 Move Semantics and R-value References

Move semantics is a feature introduced in C++11 that allows resources to be transferred (moved) from one object to another, rather than being copied. This can significantly improve performance, especially in situations where large objects (such as containers) are passed between functions.

10.1.1 R-value References

An **r-value reference** is a type of reference that can bind to temporary (r-value) objects, enabling move semantics. In contrast, **l-value references** bind to objects that persist (l-values).

- **R-value**: An expression that does not refer to a persistent object (e.g., `std::vector<int>{}` or the result of a function returning by value).
- **L-value**: An object that persists beyond a single expression (e.g., variables like `x`).
- **Syntax of r-value references**: R-value references are declared using `&&`.

cpp

```cpp
#include <iostream>
#include <vector>
using namespace std;

void foo(vector<int>&& vec) {
    cout << "Moving a vector of size: " <<
vec.size() << endl;
}

int main() {
```

```cpp
    vector<int> v = {1, 2, 3, 4, 5};
    foo(std::move(v));      // Move    v    to    foo,
transferring ownership of resources
    // v is now in a valid but unspecified state
    return 0;
}
```

In this example:

- `std::move(v)` casts v to an r-value reference, allowing it to be moved rather than copied.

10.1.2 Move Constructor and Move Assignment Operator

Move semantics are implemented through the **move constructor** and **move assignment operator**, which allow for the efficient transfer of resources.

- **Move constructor**: Transfers ownership of resources from one object to another without ing.
- **Move assignment operator**: Transfers ownership of resources during assignment.

cpp

```cpp
class MyClass {
private:
    int* data;
```

```cpp
public:
    MyClass(int value) : data(new int(value)) {}
// Regular constructor
    ~MyClass() { delete data; }

    // Move constructor
    MyClass(MyClass&&    other)    noexcept    :
data(other.data) {
        other.data = nullptr;
    }

    // Move assignment operator
    MyClass& operator=(MyClass&& other) noexcept
{
        if (this != &other) {
            delete data;   // Clean up existing
resources
            data = other.data;
            other.data = nullptr;
        }
        return *this;
    }
};
```

- The **move constructor** takes an r-value reference and moves the resource from `other` to the new object, leaving `other` in a valid but empty state.

- The **move assignment operator** does a similar operation when assigning one object to another.

10.2 Smart Pointers (unique_ptr, shared_ptr, weak_ptr)

Smart pointers are wrappers around regular pointers that automatically manage the memory they point to, making it easier to avoid memory leaks and dangling pointers. C++11 introduced several types of smart pointers in the `<memory>` header.

10.2.1 `std::unique_ptr`

A **unique_ptr** is a smart pointer that owns a dynamically allocated object exclusively. Only one `unique_ptr` can own a given object, ensuring that the object is automatically deleted when the `unique_ptr` goes out of scope.

- **Example**: Using `unique_ptr`:

cpp

```
#include <iostream>
#include <memory>
using namespace std;

class MyClass {
```

```
public:
    MyClass() { cout << "Constructor called!" <<
endl; }
    ~MyClass() { cout << "Destructor called!" <<
endl; }
};

int main() {
    unique_ptr<MyClass>           ptr1            =
make_unique<MyClass>();
    // Automatic cleanup when ptr1 goes out of
scope
    return 0;
}
```

- **Advantages**:
  - o Automatic memory management, preventing
    memory leaks.
  - o Prevents accidental copies (ing a `unique_ptr` is
    not allowed).

10.2.2 `std::shared_ptr`

A **shared_ptr** is a smart pointer that allows multiple
pointers to share ownership of a resource. The resource is
deleted when the last `shared_ptr` owning it is destroyed.

- **Example**: Using `shared_ptr`:

cpp

```cpp
#include <iostream>
#include <memory>
using namespace std;

class MyClass {
public:
    MyClass() { cout << "Constructor called!" <<
endl; }
    ~MyClass() { cout << "Destructor called!" <<
endl; }
};

int main() {
    shared_ptr<MyClass>           ptr1           =
make_shared<MyClass>();
    shared_ptr<MyClass> ptr2 = ptr1;  // ptr1 and
ptr2 share ownership

    // Destructor will be called when both ptr1
and ptr2 go out of scope
    return 0;
}
```

- **Advantages**:
  - o Automatic memory management with shared ownership.

o Prevents resource leaks when objects are shared across multiple owners.

10.2.3 `std::weak_ptr`

A **weak_ptr** is used to observe a `shared_ptr` without affecting its reference count. It does not prevent the object from being deleted.

- **Example**: Using `weak_ptr`:

cpp

```cpp
#include <iostream>
#include <memory>
using namespace std;

int main() {
    shared_ptr<int>        sharedPtr        =
make_shared<int>(10);
    weak_ptr<int> weakPtr = sharedPtr;    // Weak
reference to sharedPtr

    cout << "sharedPtr    use_count:    " <<
sharedPtr.use_count() << endl;    // Output: 1
    cout << "weakPtr    use_count:    " <<
weakPtr.use_count() << endl;        // Output: 1
```

```
sharedPtr.reset();  // sharedPtr is reset
cout << "After reset, weakPtr expired: " <<
weakPtr.expired() << endl;  // Output: 1

    return 0;
}
```

- **Advantages**:
    o Useful for observing objects managed by
      shared_ptr without preventing them from
      being deleted.

10.3 Lambda Functions and Function Objects

Lambda functions provide a concise way to define anonymous functions directly in your code. They are often used for short-lived, inline operations, such as passing functions to algorithms.

10.3.1 Lambda Functions

A **lambda function** has the following syntax:

cpp

```
[capture](parameters) -> return_type { body }
```

- **Example**: Using a lambda function:

cpp

```cpp
#include <iostream>
using namespace std;

int main() {
    auto add = [](int a, int b) { return a + b;
};
    cout << "Sum: " << add(5, 7) << endl;    // 
Output: Sum: 12
    return 0;
}
```

- **Capture list**: The [capture] part captures variables from the surrounding scope. You can capture by reference (&) or by value (=).

10.3.2 Function Objects

A **function object** (or **functor**) is a class that overloads the operator() to behave like a function.

- **Example**: Using a function object:

cpp

```cpp
#include <iostream>
using namespace std;
```

```
class Adder {
public:
    int operator()(int a, int b) {
        return a + b;
    }
};

int main() {
    Adder add;
    cout << "Sum: " << add(5, 7) << endl;    //
Output: Sum: 12
    return 0;
}
```

- **Advantages**:
    - o Function objects can maintain state, unlike
      lambdas, which are limited to capturing external
      variables.

10.4 Type Traits and Metaprogramming

Type traits and **metaprogramming** allow you to inspect
and manipulate types at compile time, which can improve
performance by making decisions during compilation rather
than runtime.

10.4.1 Type Traits

Type traits are templates that provide information about types at compile time. They are often used to create type-safe code that performs different operations depending on the type.

- **Example**: Checking if a type is an integer:

cpp

```
#include <iostream>
#include <type_traits>
using namespace std;

template <typename T>
void checkType(T value) {
    if (is_integral<T>::value) {
        cout << "The type is an integral type!" << endl;
    } else {
        cout << "The type is not an integral type!" << endl;
    }
}

int main() {
```

```
    checkType(5);     // Output: The type is an
integral type!
    checkType(3.14);  // Output: The type is not
an integral type!
    return 0;
}
```

- **std::is_integral<T>::value** is a type trait that checks if T is an integral type (e.g., int, long, char).

10.4.2 Metaprogramming

Metaprogramming involves writing programs that generate or manipulate code at compile time. **Template metaprogramming** uses templates to perform computations or generate code based on types.

- **Example**: Factorial computation at compile time:

cpp

```cpp
template <int N>
struct Factorial {
    static const int value = N * Factorial<N -
1>::value;
};

template <>
```

```cpp
struct Factorial<0> {
    static const int value = 1;  // Base case
};

int main() {
    cout << "Factorial of 5: " <<
Factorial<5>::value << endl;  // Output: 120
    return 0;
}
```

- In this example, the **Factorial** struct calculates the factorial of a number at compile time using recursion.

Conclusion

In this chapter, we covered advanced C++ features for high-performance applications. We explored **move semantics** and **r-value references**, which optimize memory usage and object transfers. **Smart pointers** like `unique_ptr`, `shared_ptr`, and `weak_ptr` help manage dynamic memory safely. We learned about **lambda functions** and **function objects**, which provide more flexibility in passing and defining functions. Finally, we explored **type traits** and **metaprogramming**, which enable compile-time optimizations and type manipulations. By mastering these advanced features, you can write more efficient, maintainable, and modern C++ code.

CHAPTER 11

COMPETITIVE PROGRAMMING WITH C++

Competitive programming involves solving algorithmic challenges within a limited time and space. Success in competitive programming requires a deep understanding of algorithms, data structures, and optimization techniques. In this chapter, we will discuss strategies for solving algorithmic problems, explore efficient data structures and algorithms, address handling large inputs and outputs, and provide real-world examples from competitive programming.

11.1 Strategies for Solving Algorithmic Problems

Effective problem-solving in competitive programming requires a structured approach. Here are some common strategies to tackle algorithmic problems:

11.1.1 Understand the Problem

The first step in solving any problem is to carefully read and understand the problem statement. Identify:

- **Inputs**: What data is given?
- **Outputs**: What should be returned?
- **Constraints**: What are the limitations (e.g., time limits, input size)?
- **Examples**: Work through the given examples to understand how the solution should behave.

11.1.2 Break the Problem into Sub-Problems

If the problem seems complex, break it down into smaller, more manageable sub-problems. This allows you to solve parts of the problem independently and combine them to form the complete solution.

11.1.3 Identify Suitable Algorithms

Once you understand the problem and have broken it down, identify which algorithms or techniques might be most suitable. Common approaches include:

- **Greedy Algorithms**: Make local optimizations in hopes of finding a global optimum.

- **Divide and Conquer**: Break the problem into smaller sub-problems, solve them recursively, and combine the solutions.

- **Dynamic Programming (DP)**: Solve problems by breaking them down into overlapping sub-problems and storing intermediate results.

- **Backtracking**: Explore all potential solutions and backtrack when a partial solution is not valid.

- **Graph Algorithms**: For problems involving graphs (e.g., shortest path, connected components, traversal).

11.1.4 Optimize for Time and Space Complexity

Time and space constraints are critical in competitive programming. After implementing the basic solution, analyze its time and space complexity:

- **Time complexity**: Focus on reducing unnecessary computations, avoid brute force, and choose algorithms with lower time complexity.

- **Space complexity**: Use memory-efficient data structures and avoid excessive space consumption.

11.1.5 Test and Debug

Once the solution is implemented, test it with different edge cases, large inputs, and potential corner cases (e.g., empty inputs, large values). Use debugging techniques like printing intermediate values to understand the flow of the program.

11.2 Efficient Data Structures and Algorithms

Efficient data structures and algorithms are essential for solving competitive programming problems within time limits. Below are some of the most useful data structures and algorithms in competitive programming.

11.2.1 Arrays and Vectors

- **Array**: An array is a fixed-size collection of elements, all of the same type. It provides fast access to elements using indices.
- **std::vector**: A dynamic array in C++ that can resize as needed. It provides more flexibility than a static array, especially when the size of the collection is not known in advance.

cpp

```
#include <iostream>
#include <vector>
using namespace std;

int main() {
```

```
vector<int> v = {1, 2, 3, 4, 5};
for (int i = 0; i < v.size(); ++i) {
    cout << v[i] << " ";   // Output: 1 2 3 4
5
}
cout << endl;
return 0;
}
```

11.2.2 Stacks and Queues

- **Stack**: A last-in-first-out (LIFO) data structure. Useful for problems that require backtracking or maintaining state (e.g., balanced parentheses).
- **Queue**: A first-in-first-out (FIFO) data structure. Useful for breadth-first search (BFS) or managing tasks in order.

cpp

```
#include <iostream>
#include <stack>
#include <queue>
using namespace std;

int main() {
    // Stack Example
    stack<int> st;
    st.push(1);
    st.push(2);
```

```cpp
    cout << st.top() << endl;   // Output: 2
    st.pop();

    // Queue Example
    queue<int> q;
    q.push(1);
    q.push(2);
    cout << q.front() << endl;   // Output: 1
    q.pop();

    return 0;
}
```

11.2.3 Hash Tables (Maps and Unordered Maps)

- **std::map**: An ordered associative container that stores key-value pairs in a sorted order (based on the keys). It supports efficient search, insertion, and deletion.
- **std::unordered_map**: An unordered associative container that stores key-value pairs using a hash table. It allows for faster average-time complexity for lookups (O(1) on average).

cpp

```cpp
#include <iostream>
#include <map>
#include <unordered_map>
using namespace std;
```

```cpp
int main() {
    // Map Example
    map<int, string> m;
    m[1] = "one";
    m[2] = "two";
    cout << m[1] << endl;  // Output: one

    // Unordered Map Example
    unordered_map<int, string> um;
    um[1] = "one";
    um[2] = "two";
    cout << um[2] << endl;  // Output: two

    return 0;
}
```

11.2.4 Sorting and Searching Algorithms

Sorting and searching algorithms are core elements in competitive programming.

- **Sorting Algorithms**: Common sorting algorithms include quicksort, mergesort, and heapsort. In C++, the standard library provides `std::sort` for efficient sorting.
- **Searching Algorithms**: Binary search is often used on sorted arrays to find elements in logarithmic time ($O(\log n)$).

cpp

```cpp
#include <iostream>
#include <vector>
#include <algorithm>  // for std::sort
using namespace std;

int main() {
    vector<int> v = {5, 3, 8, 1, 2};
    sort(v.begin(), v.end());  // Sort the vector
    for (int num : v) {
        cout << num << " ";   // Output: 1 2 3 5 8
    }
    cout << endl;
    return 0;
}
```

11.2.5 Dynamic Programming (DP)

Dynamic programming is used to solve problems that can be broken down into overlapping subproblems. By storing the results of subproblems, DP reduces the computation time for problems like the knapsack problem, longest common subsequence, and more.

- **Example**: Fibonacci sequence using DP

cpp

```cpp
#include <iostream>
#include <vector>
using namespace std;

int fibonacci(int n) {
    vector<int> dp(n + 1);
    dp[0] = 0;
    dp[1] = 1;
    for (int i = 2; i <= n; ++i) {
        dp[i] = dp[i - 1] + dp[i - 2];
    }
    return dp[n];
}

int main() {
    cout << "Fibonacci(10): " << fibonacci(10) <<
endl;   // Output: 55
    return 0;
}
```

11.2.6 Graph Algorithms

Graph algorithms are used to solve problems involving
nodes and edges, such as finding the shortest path or
detecting cycles.

- **Breadth-First Search (BFS)**: Used to explore the graph
  level by level, typically used for unweighted shortest path
  problems.
- **Depth-First Search (DFS)**: Used to explore the graph as
  deep as possible along each branch.

cpp

```cpp
#include <iostream>
#include <queue>
#include <vector>
using namespace std;

void bfs(const vector<vector<int>>& graph, int
start) {
    vector<bool> visited(graph.size(), false);
    queue<int> q;
    visited[start] = true;
    q.push(start);

    while (!q.empty()) {
        int node = q.front();
        q.pop();
        cout << node << " ";
        for (int neighbor : graph[node]) {
            if (!visited[neighbor]) {
                visited[neighbor] = true;
                q.push(neighbor);
```

```cpp
            }
        }
    }
}


int main() {
    vector<vector<int>> graph = {
        {1, 2},     // Node 0 is connected to 1
and 2
        {0, 3},     // Node 1 is connected to 0
and 3
        {0, 3},     // Node 2 is connected to 0
and 3
        {1, 2, 4}, // Node 3 is connected to 1,
2, and 4
        {3}         // Node 4 is connected to 3
    };

    cout << "BFS traversal starting from node 0:
";
    bfs(graph, 0);  // Output: 0 1 2 3 4
    cout << endl;

    return 0;
}
```

11.3 Handling Large Inputs and Outputs

In competitive programming, handling large inputs and outputs efficiently is crucial to meet the time constraints. Here are a few strategies for efficiently dealing with large I/O:

11.3.1 Fast Input/Output

Using standard input/output functions in C++ can be slow, especially when handling large datasets. Using `cin` and `cout` may not be fast enough, so we can use faster alternatives.

- **Faster Input**: Using `scanf` and `printf` for faster input/output in some cases.
- **Using** `ios::sync_with_stdio(false)`: This disables the synchronization between C++ standard streams (`cin`, `cout`) and C standard streams (`stdio`), which can improve performance.

cpp

```cpp
#include <iostream>
#include <cstdio>
using namespace std;

int main() {
```

```cpp
    ios::sync_with_stdio(false);      // Disable
synchronization with C streams
    cin.tie(0);  // Unlink cin from cout to avoid
flushing
    int n;
    cin >> n;
    cout << "Number: " << n << endl;
    return 0;
}
```

11.3.2 Reading Large Inputs

For reading large datasets efficiently, you can read input in bulk and then process it.

cpp

```cpp
#include <iostream>
#include <vector>
using namespace std;

int main() {
    int n;
    cin >> n;
    vector<int> data(n);
    for (int i = 0; i < n; ++i) {
        cin >> data[i];
    }

    // Processing data
```

```cpp
for (int i = 0; i < n; ++i) {
    cout << data[i] << " ";
}
cout << endl;
return 0;
}
```

11.4 Real-World Examples from Competitive Programming

Here are a few typical examples of algorithmic problems you might encounter in competitive programming:

1. **Knapsack Problem**: Dynamic programming is used to maximize the total value of items that can fit within a fixed weight capacity.

2. **Shortest Path Algorithms**: Dijkstra's algorithm or Bellman-Ford algorithm can be used to find the shortest path in a weighted graph.

3. **Maximum Subarray Sum**: Kadane's algorithm can efficiently solve this problem in $O(n)$ time.

4. **Finding Connected Components**: DFS or BFS can be used to find connected components in an undirected graph.

Conclusion

In this chapter, we explored key concepts in **competitive programming with C++**. We discussed strategies for solving algorithmic problems, the importance of efficient data structures and algorithms, and handling large inputs and outputs efficiently. By understanding these concepts and practicing different types of problems, you can improve your competitive programming skills and prepare for contests or challenges.

CHAPTER 12

C++ IN GAME DEVELOPMENT

C++ is one of the most popular languages in game development due to its high performance, control over system resources, and support for object-oriented programming. In this chapter, we will discuss C++'s role in game development, focusing on **game engine architecture**, **graphics programming** with OpenGL or DirectX, **game loops, physics engines**, and **optimization for real-time performance**.

12.1 Game Engine Architecture and C++'s Role

A **game engine** is a software framework used to create and develop video games. It provides the essential tools for handling rendering, physics, sound, input, and other aspects of game development. C++ plays a crucial role in game engine development due to its speed, low-level memory control, and ability to interact with hardware efficiently.

12.1.1 Key Components of a Game Engine

- **Rendering Engine**: Handles the graphics rendering, including 2D and 3D graphics. This component is responsible for drawing objects on the screen.

- **Physics Engine**: Simulates the physical interactions in the game, including collision detection, rigid body dynamics, and gravity.

- **Audio Engine**: Manages sound effects and music, providing an immersive experience for the player.

- **Input System**: Captures input from the player (keyboard, mouse, gamepad) and translates it into actions in the game.

- **Scripting**: Allows the game logic to be programmed using higher-level scripting languages, often integrated with C++.

- **Networking**: Handles online multiplayer functionality and data synchronization.

12.1.2 C++ in Game Engine Architecture

C++ is often used in the core components of a game engine for several reasons:

- **Performance**: C++ provides direct access to hardware and low-level system resources, ensuring that the engine runs efficiently, especially in resource-intensive tasks such as graphics rendering and physics simulation.

- **Memory Management**: C++ allows developers to have precise control over memory allocation, which is critical for performance in games with large amounts of data (e.g., textures, models, animations).

- **Object-Oriented Programming**: C++ supports OOP, which is useful for creating modular, reusable game components (e.g., entities, game objects, scenes).

12.2 Graphics Programming with OpenGL or DirectX

Graphics programming is a central aspect of game development. **OpenGL** and **DirectX** are two of the most commonly used graphics APIs for creating high-quality visual effects in games.

12.2.1 OpenGL

OpenGL (Open Graphics Library) is an open-source, cross-platform graphics API used for rendering 2D and 3D graphics. It provides a set of functions for drawing shapes, manipulating textures, and applying lighting effects.

- **Example**: Simple OpenGL program to render a triangle:

cpp

```cpp
#include <GL/glut.h>   // OpenGL Utility Toolkit
(GLUT) library

void display() {
    glClear(GL_COLOR_BUFFER_BIT);   // Clear the
screen

    // Set color to red
    glColor3f(1.0, 0.0, 0.0);

    // Draw a triangle
    glBegin(GL_TRIANGLES);
        glVertex2f(-0.5f, -0.5f);
        glVertex2f(0.5f, -0.5f);
        glVertex2f(0.0f, 0.5f);
    glEnd();

    glFlush();   // Render the graphics
}

int main(int argc, char **argv) {
    glutInit(&argc, argv);
    glutInitDisplayMode(GLUT_SINGLE | GLUT_RGB);
    glutInitWindowSize(500, 500);
    glutCreateWindow("OpenGL Triangle");
    glutDisplayFunc(display);
    glutMainLoop();        // Enter the event-
processing loop
```

```
    return 0;
}
```

- **Key OpenGL Functions**:
    o `glBegin(GL_TRIANGLES)`: Starts defining a shape (in this case, a triangle).
    o `glVertex2f(x, y)`: Defines a vertex for the shape.
    o `glColor3f(r, g, b)`: Sets the color for the shape.

12.2.2 DirectX

DirectX is a collection of APIs developed by Microsoft, designed specifically for Windows-based games. DirectX includes components for graphics (Direct3D), sound (DirectSound), input (DirectInput), and more.

- **Direct3D**: The core of DirectX for rendering 3D graphics.
- **HLSL (High-Level Shader Language)**: Used in DirectX for writing shaders, which are small programs that run on the GPU to handle tasks like rendering and post-processing.
- **Example**: Direct3D code typically involves initializing the graphics device, setting up a

165

viewport, defining a camera, and rendering objects with shaders. A full example is extensive and requires a setup of DirectX SDK tools, which might not fit within a simple snippet.

12.2.3 Differences Between OpenGL and DirectX

- **Cross-Platform Support**: OpenGL is cross-platform and can be used on Windows, Linux, and macOS, while DirectX is limited to Windows platforms.
- **Performance**: DirectX often provides better optimization for Windows-based games, as it's tightly integrated with the operating system.
- **Ease of Use**: OpenGL is often considered simpler to use for beginners, whereas DirectX offers more advanced features for high-performance game development.

12.3 Game Loops and Physics Engines

12.3.1 Game Loops

A **game loop** is the core of a real-time game. It runs continuously, processing input, updating the game state, and rendering the game world to the screen. The game loop typically includes the following stages:

1. **Process Input**: Handle user input (e.g., keyboard, mouse, gamepad).

2. **Update Game State**: Update game objects, physics, and logic.

3. **Render**: Draw the updated game world to the screen.

4. **Repeat**: The loop repeats at a fixed rate to ensure smooth gameplay.

- **Example**: A basic game loop structure:

cpp

```cpp
#include <iostream>
#include <chrono>
#include <thread>
using namespace std;

void processInput() {
    // Handle input (keyboard, mouse, etc.)
}

void updateGame() {
    // Update game logic, physics, etc.
}

void render() {
    // Render graphics to the screen
}
```

```cpp
int main() {
    while (true) {
        auto                    start           =
chrono::high_resolution_clock::now();

        processInput();
        updateGame();
        render();

        auto                end             =
chrono::high_resolution_clock::now();
        chrono::duration<float> elapsed = end -
start;

        // Ensure the game loop runs at 60 frames
per second

this_thread::sleep_for(chrono::milliseconds(16)
- elapsed);   // 1000ms / 60 = 16.67ms per frame
    }
    return 0;
}
```

- **Frame Rate Independence**: The game loop runs at a fixed rate (e.g., 60 FPS) to ensure smooth gameplay across different hardware. The sleep_for function ensures the loop runs at a constant speed.

12.3.2 Physics Engines

A **physics engine** simulates realistic movements and interactions in the game world, including gravity, collision detection, and response.

- **Common Physics Engines**:
    - **Box2D**: A 2D physics engine commonly used in 2D games.
    - **Bullet**: A 3D physics engine used in physics-heavy simulations and games.
    - **Havok**: A commercial physics engine used in many AAA games.

Physics engines rely on algorithms for collision detection (e.g., bounding boxes, spheres) and rigid body dynamics (e.g., Newton's laws of motion).

- **Example**: A simple physics update in a game might involve applying forces (like gravity) to an object and updating its position:

cpp

```cpp
struct Vector2 {
    float x, y;
};
```

```cpp
struct Object {
    Vector2 position;
    Vector2 velocity;
};

void updatePhysics(Object& obj, float deltaTime)
{
    const float gravity = -9.81f;
    obj.velocity.y += gravity * deltaTime;    // Apply gravity
    obj.position.x += obj.velocity.x * deltaTime;    // Update position based on velocity
    obj.position.y += obj.velocity.y * deltaTime;
}
```

12.4 Optimization for Real-Time Performance

Real-time performance is crucial for game development, especially for action-oriented or graphically intensive games. To ensure smooth gameplay, various optimization techniques are applied:

12.4.1 Reducing Draw Calls

- **Draw Calls**: Each time the CPU sends a command to the GPU to render a new object, it generates a draw call.

Minimizing the number of draw calls can improve
performance.

- **Instancing**: When rendering many copies of the same
object, use **instancing** to draw multiple objects with a
single draw call.

12.4.2 Level of Detail (LOD)

- **Level of Detail**: Adjust the complexity of rendered
objects based on their distance from the camera. Objects
far from the player can be rendered with lower detail to
save performance.

12.4.3 Culling

- **Frustum Culling**: Avoid rendering objects outside of the
camera's view by performing frustum culling, which
eliminates objects that are not visible.
- **Occlusion Culling**: Similarly, avoid rendering objects
that are blocked by other objects.

12.4.4 Multi-threading and Parallelism

- **Multi-threading**: Use multiple threads to offload
independent tasks (e.g., loading assets, physics, AI) from
the main game loop, ensuring that the game loop remains
smooth.

- **GPU Acceleration**: Offload heavy computations, such as physics simulations and rendering, to the GPU using shaders and compute pipelines.

12.4.5 Memory Management

- **Memory Pooling**: Use memory pools to allocate and deallocate memory efficiently, avoiding costly dynamic memory allocations during runtime.
- **Garbage Collection**: In some game engines, avoid frequent garbage collection (common in higher-level languages) by managing memory manually or using custom memory allocators.

Conclusion

C++ is integral to modern game development, providing the power and control needed for building high-performance game engines. In this chapter, we covered game engine architecture and C++'s role in it, graphics programming with OpenGL or DirectX, the importance of game loops and physics engines, and optimization techniques for real-time performance. By mastering these advanced game development topics, you can build highly efficient, immersive games that run smoothly on a variety of platforms.

CHAPTER 13

C++ FOR SYSTEM PROGRAMMING

System programming involves developing software that interacts directly with hardware or provides foundational services to other software. C++ is widely used in system programming due to its low-level memory control, efficiency, and ability to interface with hardware. This chapter covers low-level programming with C++, writing system utilities and drivers, handling input/output operations and file management, and using C++ for real-time systems and embedded applications.

13.1 Low-level Programming with C++

Low-level programming involves working closely with the hardware, managing memory manually, and directly interacting with system resources. C++ allows developers to write efficient, high-performance code that interacts directly with the underlying system.

13.1.1 Memory Management

One of the core features of C++ in system programming is manual memory management. Unlike languages with automatic garbage collection, C++ gives developers full control over memory allocation and deallocation using pointers.

- **Dynamic Memory Allocation**: Use `new` and `delete` to allocate and free memory on the heap.

cpp

```cpp
int* ptr = new int(10);   // Allocate memory for
an integer
cout << *ptr << endl;     // Output: 10
delete ptr;               // Free memory
```

- **Memory Management in Arrays**: C++ also provides support for dynamic arrays through `new[]` and `delete[]`.

cpp

```cpp
int* arr = new int[5];   // Allocate an array of
5 integers
for (int i = 0; i < 5; ++i) {
```

```
    arr[i] = i * i;        // Assign values to the
array
}
delete[] arr;   // Free the allocated array
```

13.1.2 Pointers and Direct Memory Access

Pointers allow you to reference and manipulate memory addresses directly. In system programming, pointers are often used to work with hardware registers, memory-mapped I/O, and buffers.

- **Pointer Arithmetic**: This is often used in low-level programming to traverse through arrays or buffers.

cpp

```
int arr[] = {1, 2, 3, 4, 5};
int* ptr = arr;
cout << *(ptr + 2) << endl;   // Output: 3
(Accessing the 3rd element in the array)
```

- **Memory-mapped I/O**: Many embedded systems and hardware devices expose memory-mapped I/O for controlling peripherals. Using pointers, you can access these I/O regions directly.

cpp

```
volatile       int*       control_register      =
reinterpret_cast<volatile int*>(0x40001000);   //
Memory-mapped I/O address
*control_register = 1;    // Write to control
register
```

13.1.3 Assembly Integration

C++ can be used alongside assembly code to achieve low-level control over hardware. Inline assembly allows for executing assembly instructions directly in a C++ program.

cpp

```cpp
#include <iostream>
using namespace std;

int main() {
    int result;
    __asm {
        MOV EAX, 5  // Load 5 into EAX register
        MOV result, EAX  // Store value of EAX
into result
    }
    cout << "Result: " << result << endl;   //
Output: Result: 5
    return 0;
}
```

This code uses inline assembly to load a value into a register and store it in a C++ variable.

13.2 Writing System Utilities and Drivers

System utilities and drivers are essential components of an operating system or embedded system. They allow the OS to interact with hardware devices and provide services to higher-level applications.

13.2.1 Writing System Utilities

System utilities are programs that perform tasks such as process management, memory management, and file system management. C++ is well-suited for writing these utilities due to its efficiency and control over system resources.

- **Example**: A simple utility to list files in a directory (platform-dependent).

cpp

```cpp
#include <iostream>
#include <filesystem>
namespace fs = std::filesystem;

int main() {
```

```cpp
    for      (const      auto&      entry      :
fs::directory_iterator(".")) {
        std::cout << entry.path() << std::endl;
    }
    return 0;
}
```

This utility uses the C++17 filesystem library to list all files in the current directory.

13.2.2 Writing Drivers

A **device driver** is a program that allows the operating system to communicate with hardware devices. C++ is often used to write drivers for embedded systems, hardware peripherals, and custom devices.

- **Example**: Writing a simple device driver might involve using C++ in conjunction with system-specific APIs, such as those provided by Linux (sysfs, udev) or Windows (WDM).

cpp

```cpp
// Pseudocode   for   writing   a   simple   driver
interface in C++
#include <iostream>
```

```cpp
void writeToDevice(int data) {
    // Interact with hardware by writing data to
a specific memory-mapped register
    volatile    int*    device_register    =
reinterpret_cast<volatile int*>(0x40000000);
    *device_register = data;
}

int main() {
    writeToDevice(42);   // Write the value 42 to
the device
    return 0;
}
```

In real drivers, you would need to interface with kernel-mode APIs and ensure that the driver is loaded and initialized correctly within the operating system.

13.3 Handling Input/Output Operations and File Management

Handling I/O operations efficiently is essential for system programming. C++ provides a rich set of tools for working with files and interacting with the user.

13.3.1 File Handling

C++ provides both **stream-based** I/O and **C-style** file I/O. The standard library supports reading and writing files using `fstream`.

- **File input/output with `fstream`:**

cpp

```cpp
#include <iostream>
#include <fstream>
#include <string>
using namespace std;

int main() {
    ofstream outFile("output.txt");
    outFile << "Hello, C++ File I/O!" << endl;
    outFile.close();

    ifstream inFile("output.txt");
    string line;
    while (getline(inFile, line)) {
        cout << line << endl;  // Output: Hello,
C++ File I/O!
    }
    inFile.close();
    return 0;
```

```
}
```

- **Error Handling**: C++ provides mechanisms for error handling during file operations, such as checking if a file was successfully opened using `ifstream::is_open()` or `ofstream::is_open()`.

13.3.2 Low-level File I/O

For more control over file I/O, such as binary files or memory-mapped files, C++ allows you to use low-level system calls or POSIX-style I/O operations.

- **Example**: Reading a binary file using `open()`, `read()`, and `close()` on Linux:

cpp

```cpp
#include <iostream>
#include <fcntl.h>
#include <unistd.h>
using namespace std;

int main() {
    int file = open("binary.dat", O_RDONLY);
    if (file == -1) {
        perror("Error opening file");
        return 1;
```

```
    }

    char buffer[100];
    ssize_t  bytesRead  =  read(file,  buffer,
sizeof(buffer));
    if (bytesRead == -1) {
        perror("Error reading file");
        close(file);
        return 1;
    }

    cout.write(buffer, bytesRead);
    close(file);
    return 0;
}
```

This demonstrates low-level file handling using file descriptors in a system programming context.

13.4 Real-Time Systems and Embedded Applications

Real-time systems are systems that must respond to inputs within a guaranteed time frame. C++ is commonly used for embedded systems and real-time applications due to its high performance and low overhead.

13.4.1 Real-Time Systems

A **real-time system** must meet timing constraints, often referred to as deadlines. For example, an embedded system controlling a robot may need to process sensor data and respond within a specified time limit.

- **Example**: In a real-time system, C++ can be used to manage timing, scheduling, and task synchronization. For instance, you could use `std::this_thread::sleep_for()` to introduce a delay or control timing between operations.

cpp

```cpp
#include <iostream>
#include <thread>
using namespace std;

void realTimeTask() {
    while (true) {
        // Simulate a task
        cout << "Performing task..." << endl;

this_thread::sleep_for(chrono::milliseconds(50)
);  // Control timing
    }
}
```

```cpp
int main() {
    thread taskThread(realTimeTask);
    taskThread.join();    // Start the real-time task
    return 0;
}
```

13.4.2 Embedded Systems

Embedded systems are specialized computing systems designed to perform dedicated tasks. C++ is frequently used for developing embedded applications, such as firmware for microcontrollers and systems that interface directly with hardware.

- **Example**: Programming an embedded system typically involves working with specific hardware libraries or APIs. For example, controlling an LED on a microcontroller might look like this in a simplified example:

cpp

```cpp
#include <iostream>
using namespace std;

// Pseudocode for embedded LED control
```

```cpp
void turnOnLED() {
    // Set a register or GPIO pin to HIGH
    cout << "LED turned ON!" << endl;
}

void turnOffLED() {
    // Set a register or GPIO pin to LOW
    cout << "LED turned OFF!" << endl;
}

int main() {
    turnOnLED();
    this_thread::sleep_for(chrono::seconds(1));
// Wait for 1 second
    turnOffLED();
    return 0;
}
```

In embedded systems, you would be working with microcontroller-specific libraries (such as Arduino or STM32) to control hardware directly.

Conclusion

In this chapter, we explored **C++ for system programming** and its role in low-level programming, system utilities, and driver development. We discussed techniques for **handling input/output operations**, **file management**, and working

185

with **real-time systems** and **embedded applications**. C++'s efficiency, control over hardware, and ability to interact with low-level system resources make it an ideal language for system programming tasks. By understanding these techniques, you can effectively develop software that interacts closely with hardware and provides essential services to other applications.

CHAPTER 14

BEST PRACTICES FOR WRITING MAINTAINABLE C++ CODE

Writing maintainable C++ code is essential for long-term success in software development. As projects grow in size and complexity, ensuring that your code is readable, efficient, reusable, and well-tested becomes crucial. This chapter focuses on best practices for writing maintainable C++ code, including code readability, organization, writing clean and efficient code, error handling, exceptions, and debugging techniques.

14.1 Code Readability and Organization

Code readability is one of the most important aspects of maintainable code. Code that is easy to read, understand, and modify reduces the likelihood of bugs and makes it easier for developers to collaborate on a project.

14.1.1 Consistent Naming Conventions

- **Variables and functions**: Use meaningful names that clearly convey the purpose of the variable or function.
  - Use camelCase for variable names (e.g., `studentName`) and snake_case for function names (e.g., `calculate_average()`).
  - Avoid single-letter variable names (except for loop indices) and cryptic names.
- **Classes and types**: Use PascalCase for class and type names (e.g., `StudentData`), and clearly define the type's purpose.
- **Constants**: Use uppercase letters with underscores for constants (e.g., `MAX_BUFFER_SIZE`).

14.1.2 Organizing Code into Logical Units

- **Functions**: Keep functions short and focused on a single task. A function should ideally perform one thing and do it well.
- **Classes**: Group related functions and data members into classes. A class should represent a single concept or entity.
- **Files**: Organize code into separate files based on their functionality. Typically, header files (`.h` or `.hpp`) contain

declarations, while source files (`.cpp`) contain definitions.

- o Example structure:

```css
src/
    main.cpp
    student.cpp
    student.h
```

14.1.3 Consistent Indentation and Formatting

Use consistent indentation (preferably 4 spaces) to structure the code, making it easy to read and follow. Most IDEs and text editors have automatic formatting tools or plugins for C++ (e.g., `clang-format`).

- **Braces**: Use the same style for braces, preferably placing the opening brace on the same line as the function declaration or control structure.

```cpp
if (condition) {
    // Code block
}
```

- **Line Length**: Keep line length under a reasonable limit (usually 80 or 100 characters) to avoid horizontal scrolling.

14.2 Writing Clean, Efficient, and Reusable Code

Writing clean code means ensuring that your code is simple, efficient, and reusable. Efficient code avoids unnecessary computations, while reusable code minimizes duplication and maximizes modularity.

14.2.1 Avoiding Redundancy

- **DRY Principle** (Don't Repeat Yourself): Avoid repeating code. Instead, use functions, classes, or templates to centralize logic that can be reused.
- **Reusability**: Write functions and classes that can be reused in different contexts. For example, a sorting function should work for any type of container, not just one specific list or array.

14.2.2 Use of Smart Pointers

- Instead of manually managing memory with `new` and `delete`, use **smart pointers** (`std::unique_ptr`, `std::shared_ptr`, and `std::weak_ptr`) to automatically manage memory and prevent memory leaks.

cpp

```cpp
#include <memory>

void createObject() {
    std::unique_ptr<int>        ptr        =
std::make_unique<int>(10);
    // Automatic cleanup when ptr goes out of
scope
}
```

14.2.3 Avoiding Premature Optimization

- **Focus on readability and simplicity first**, and only optimize when performance bottlenecks are identified (e.g., after profiling). Premature optimization can make the code more complex without significant performance gains.

- **Use appropriate algorithms** and data structures to improve performance, but only after profiling the application to identify the actual bottlenecks.

14.2.4 Encapsulation and Abstraction

- **Encapsulate details**: Hide the internal details of a class and expose only necessary methods. This improves maintainability by reducing the impact of internal changes on other parts of the program.
- **Abstract common functionality**: Use abstract classes or interfaces to define common behavior, which can then be implemented in concrete classes.

cpp

```cpp
class Shape {
public:
    virtual void draw() const = 0;   // Pure
virtual function
    virtual ~Shape() = default;
};


class Circle : public Shape {
public:
    void draw() const override {
        // Draw a circle
    }
};
```

14.3 Error Handling and Exceptions

Error handling ensures that your program behaves correctly and predictably, even when something goes wrong. C++ provides mechanisms like **exceptions** to handle runtime errors.

14.3.1 Using Exceptions for Error Handling

Use **exceptions** to handle errors instead of relying on return codes or global variables.

- **Throwing exceptions**: When an error is encountered, throw an exception to indicate that something went wrong.

cpp

```cpp
#include <stdexcept>

void processData(int data) {
    if (data < 0) {
        throw    std::invalid_argument("Negative
data is not allowed.");
    }
    // Process data
}
```

- **Catching exceptions**: Use `try-catch` blocks to catch and handle exceptions.

cpp

```cpp
try {
    processData(-1);
} catch (const std::invalid_argument& e) {
    std::cerr << "Error: " << e.what() <<
std::endl;
}
```

14.3.2 Catching Specific Exceptions

- **Catching specific exceptions**: Catch specific types of exceptions (e.g., `std::out_of_range`, `std::runtime_error`) to handle different error cases in a tailored way.

cpp

```cpp
try {
    // Code that may throw exceptions
} catch (const std::out_of_range& e) {
    std::cerr << "Out of range: " << e.what() <<
std::endl;
} catch (const std::exception& e) {
    std::cerr << "Standard exception: " <<
e.what() << std::endl;
```

194

```
}
```

14.3.3 Exception Safety

Ensure your code is **exception-safe** by following one of these guidelines:

- **Basic guarantee**: The program will continue executing even if an exception is thrown, and objects are left in a valid state.
- **Strong guarantee**: The program guarantees that if an exception occurs, no changes will be made (i.e., the operation is atomic).

14.4 Unit Testing and Debugging Techniques

Testing and debugging are crucial aspects of maintaining high-quality code. By writing tests and debugging effectively, you ensure that your code behaves as expected and identify problems early in development.

14.4.1 Unit Testing

Unit testing involves writing tests for individual components (functions, classes) to ensure that they work as expected. C++ has several libraries for unit testing, such as **Google Test** and **Catch2**.

- **Example**: Using Google Test to test a function:

cpp

```cpp
#include <gtest/gtest.h>

int add(int a, int b) {
    return a + b;
}

TEST(AddTest, PositiveNumbers) {
    EXPECT_EQ(add(2, 3), 5);
}

TEST(AddTest, NegativeNumbers) {
    EXPECT_EQ(add(-2, -3), -5);
}

int main(int argc, char **argv) {
    ::testing::InitGoogleTest(&argc, argv);
    return RUN_ALL_TESTS();
}
```

- **Test-driven development (TDD)**: Write your tests before writing the actual code to ensure that each part of the program works as expected and remains maintainable.

14.4.2 Debugging Techniques

Debugging is the process of finding and fixing bugs in your code. C++ provides several tools and techniques for effective debugging:

- **Use a debugger**: Debuggers like **gdb** allow you to inspect the state of the program at runtime, set breakpoints, and step through the code.
    - Set breakpoints: Pause the program at a specific line to inspect the values of variables and the program's state.
    - Step through the code: Execute the program line by line to understand its flow and identify where errors occur.
- **Use logging**: Use logging libraries or simple `std::cout` statements to track the program's execution, output values, and identify where things go wrong.
- **Static analysis tools**: Tools like **Clang Static Analyzer** or **Cppcheck** help identify bugs, memory leaks, and other issues without running the program.
- **Assertions**: Use `assert()` to validate assumptions in your code. If the condition in the assertion is false, the program will terminate, indicating an error.

cpp

```cpp
#include <cassert>

void processData(int data) {
    assert(data >= 0);   // Assert that data is
non-negative
    // Process data
}
```

Conclusion

In this chapter, we explored best practices for writing maintainable C++ code. We emphasized the importance of **code readability** and **organization**, maintaining **clean and efficient code**, and using proper **error handling** and **exceptions**. We also discussed techniques for **unit testing** and **debugging**, which are critical for ensuring the reliability and stability of the codebase. By adhering to these practices, you can write C++ code that is not only high-performance but also robust, understandable, and easy to maintain.

CHAPTER 15

C++ AND MODERN DEVELOPMENT TOOLS

In modern C++ development, leveraging the right tools can significantly improve productivity, streamline workflows, and help you write cleaner, more efficient code. This chapter focuses on essential tools for C++ development, including **Integrated Development Environments (IDEs)**, **build systems** like CMake and Makefiles, **version control with Git**, and **debugging tools and techniques**.

15.1 Integrated Development Environments (IDEs) for C++

An **Integrated Development Environment (IDE)** combines multiple tools for software development into a single platform. IDEs for C++ provide features such as code editing, compiling, debugging, and project management to streamline the development process.

15.1.1 Popular C++ IDEs

- **Visual Studio**: One of the most powerful IDEs for C++ development, especially on Windows. It provides an integrated compiler, debugger, and GUI designer, along with a rich set of tools for performance profiling and static analysis.
  - o **Key Features**:
    - IntelliSense (autocompletion and code suggestions).
    - Integrated debugger.
    - Project templates for various C++ frameworks.
    - GUI design tools (Windows applications).
- **CLion**: Developed by JetBrains, CLion is a cross-platform IDE for C++ development that supports CMake, a build system that works seamlessly with C++ projects. CLion offers features such as code refactoring, a powerful debugger, and integration with version control systems like Git.
  - o **Key Features**:
    - Built-in CMake support.
    - Smart code analysis and navigation.
    - Refactoring tools.

- Cross-platform support (Windows, macOS, Linux).

- **Eclipse CDT (C++ Development Tools)**: A popular open-source IDE for C++ development, especially on Linux. Eclipse provides project management, syntax highlighting, debugging, and a vast ecosystem of plugins.
  - **Key Features**:
    - Highly customizable through plugins.
    - Cross-platform (Windows, macOS, Linux).
    - Supports multiple compilers and build systems.

- **Xcode**: The go-to IDE for macOS and iOS development, Xcode also supports C++ development. It integrates with Clang, Apple's compiler, and provides excellent debugging tools.
  - **Key Features**:
    - Integrated debugging and performance tools.
    - Support for Apple-specific C++ frameworks and libraries.

15.1.2 IDE Features That Enhance Productivity

- **Code Autocompletion**: Modern IDEs like Visual Studio and CLion provide autocompletion for C++ syntax, classes, functions, and variables, which speeds up coding and reduces errors.

- **Syntax Highlighting**: IDEs use color coding to distinguish different parts of the code (keywords, variables, functions, etc.), making the code easier to read.

- **Refactoring Tools**: These tools allow you to change variable names, function names, or restructure code without breaking the functionality.

- **Code Navigation**: Easily jump to a function definition, class declaration, or any part of the codebase through features like "Go to Definition" or "Find Usage".

- **Integrated Debugger**: A debugger integrated within the IDE allows for step-by-step execution, inspection of variables, breakpoints, and stack trace analysis.

15.2 Build Systems (CMake, Makefiles)

A **build system** automates the process of compiling source code into an executable or library. Build systems are crucial for managing complex projects, especially when dealing with multiple files, dependencies, and configurations.

15.2.1 CMake

CMake is a cross-platform build system generator widely used in C++ projects. Instead of writing platform-specific Makefiles, you write CMakeLists.txt files, and CMake generates the appropriate build files for your platform (e.g., Makefiles, Visual Studio project files).

- **Example CMakeLists.txt** for a simple C++ project:

```cmake
cmake_minimum_required(VERSION 3.10)

project(MyProject)

set(CMAKE_CXX_STANDARD 17)

add_executable(my_program main.cpp)
```

- **Key Features**:
    - **Cross-platform**: CMake works on Windows, Linux, macOS, and other platforms.
    - **Dependency Management**: CMake can find and link libraries automatically (e.g., Boost, OpenGL).

o **Build Configuration**: CMake can generate build files for different environments, making it easier to manage large, complex projects.

15.2.2 Makefiles

A **Makefile** is a build script used by the `make` utility, common in Linux-based C++ development. It defines rules for compiling and linking code, specifying dependencies between source files, and optimizing the build process.

- **Example Makefile**:

```
makefile
```

```
CC = g++
CFLAGS = -std=c++17 -Wall

SRC = main.cpp
OBJ = $(SRC:.cpp=.o)
EXEC = my_program

$(EXEC): $(OBJ)
    $(CC) $(OBJ) -o $(EXEC)

.cpp.o:
    $(CC) $(CFLAGS) -c $< -o $@
```

```
clean:
    rm -f $(OBJ) $(EXEC)
```

- **Key Features**:
  - o **Dependency Tracking**: `make` rebuilds only the files that have changed, making it efficient for large projects.
  - o **Customizable Rules**: You can define custom compilation, linking, and cleaning rules.
  - o **Simple and Powerful**: While not as advanced as CMake, Makefiles are a good choice for small to medium-sized projects.

15.3 Version Control with Git in C++ Projects

Version control systems (VCS) are essential for managing changes to code over time, especially when working in teams. **Git** is the most widely used version control system in modern software development.

15.3.1 Git Basics

- **Git Repository**: A Git repository stores the history of your project and tracks changes over time.
- **Git Commands**:
  - o `git init`: Initializes a new Git repository.

- o `git clone <repo>`: Clones an existing repository.

- o `git add <file>`: Adds changes to the staging area.

- o `git commit -m "message"`: Commits staged changes with a message.

- o `git push`: Pushes committed changes to a remote repository (e.g., GitHub, GitLab).

- o `git pull`: Pulls the latest changes from a remote repository.

15.3.2 Git Workflow for C++ Projects

- **Branching**: Use Git branches to work on new features, fixes, or experiments without affecting the main codebase.

  - o Example: Create a feature branch and switch between branches:

    bash

    ```bash
    git checkout -b new_feature
    git checkout main
    ```

- **Commit Early and Often**: Regular commits with descriptive messages make it easier to track changes and rollback when necessary.

- **Collaborating with Teams**: Use pull requests (PRs) to review and merge code changes before they are added to the main branch.

15.3.3 Using Git with C++ Projects

- **Large Binary Files**: C++ projects often have large binary files (e.g., object files, executables, images). Use .gitignore to exclude unnecessary files from version control.
    - o   Example .gitignore for a C++ project:

    bash

    ```
    *.o
    *.exe
    *.out
    /bin/
    /build/
    ```

- **Submodules**: If your C++ project depends on external libraries, Git submodules allow you to include other repositories as part of your project.

15.4 Debugging Tools and Techniques

Debugging is an essential part of development. C++
provides various tools and techniques to help identify and fix
issues in your code.

15.4.1 Debuggers

- **gdb (GNU Debugger)**: A powerful debugger that
  works with compiled programs in C++. gdb allows
  you to inspect the state of your program, step through
  code, and check variable values at runtime.
  - **Basic gdb commands**:
    - `gdb ./my_program`: Start the debugger
      with the compiled program.
    - `break main`: Set a breakpoint at the
      `main` function.
    - `run`: Start running the program in the
      debugger.
    - `step`: Step through the program line by
      line.
    - `print var`: Print the value of a variable.
- **Visual Studio Debugger**: If using Visual Studio, the
  built-in debugger provides an intuitive interface for

setting breakpoints, watching variables, and inspecting the call stack.

15.4.2 Static Analysis Tools

- **Cppcheck**: A static analysis tool that helps detect potential errors, code smells, and bad practices in C++ code.
- **Clang Static Analyzer**: A tool for finding bugs and vulnerabilities in C++ code, which can be integrated into the build process.

15.4.3 Memory Debugging

- **Valgrind**: A tool that helps detect memory leaks, memory corruption, and invalid memory access.
  - Example:

  ```bash
  valgrind          --leak-check=full
  ./my_program
  ```

- **AddressSanitizer**: A fast memory error detector that can catch out-of-bounds accesses, use-after-free errors, and more.

15.4.4 Profiling and Performance Analysis

- **gprof**: A profiler that helps identify performance bottlenecks in your program by analyzing function call frequencies and execution times.
- **perf**: A Linux tool that provides detailed performance profiling, including CPU cycles, cache misses, and more.

Conclusion

In this chapter, we explored the tools and practices that modern C++ developers use to improve productivity, maintainability, and code quality. We covered **Integrated Development Environments (IDEs)**, which streamline development, and **build systems** like CMake and Makefiles, which automate the compilation process. We also discussed the importance of **version control with Git** for collaboration and code management. Finally, we delved into debugging tools and techniques, which are crucial for identifying and resolving issues in C++ projects. By using these modern development tools, you can significantly enhance the efficiency and quality of your C++ projects.

CHAPTER 16

INTEGRATING C++ WITH OTHER LANGUAGES

In modern software development, it is common to integrate C++ with other programming languages to leverage the strengths of each language. C++ provides high performance, system-level access, and control over resources, while other languages like Python, Java, .NET, and web technologies provide ease of use, rapid development, and high-level abstractions. This chapter covers how to integrate C++ with other languages, including **C++ and Python integration**, **calling C++ from Java and .NET**, **using C++ in web development**, and **Foreign Function Interfaces (FFI)**.

16.1 C++ and Python Integration

Python is widely used for rapid development, scripting, and scientific computing, while C++ is used for performance-critical parts of a program. Integrating C++ with Python allows you to take advantage of C++'s speed while retaining Python's ease of use.

16.1.1 Using C++ in Python with ctypes and Cython

- **ctypes**: Python's ctypes library provides a way to call C functions and access shared libraries from Python. You can expose C++ functions via C interfaces and call them from Python.

- **Example**: Exposing a simple C++ function via a shared library and calling it in Python using ctypes:

1. **C++ Code (mylib.cpp)**:

cpp

```cpp
#include <iostream>
extern "C" {
    void hello() {
        std::cout << "Hello from C++!" << std::endl;
    }
}
```

2. **Compiling C++ Code into Shared Library**:

bash

```bash
g++ -shared -o mylib.so -fPIC mylib.cpp
```

3. **Python Code**:

```python
python

import ctypes

# Load the shared library
mylib = ctypes.CDLL('./mylib.so')

# Call the hello function
mylib.hello()
```

- **Cython**: Cython is another way to integrate C++ with Python. It allows you to write Python code that calls C and C++ functions directly, while providing performance benefits from compiling down to C.

```python
python

# Using Cython to wrap C++ code
# In a .pyx file
cdef extern from "mylib.h":
    void hello()

def call_hello():
    hello()
```

16.1.2 Python Bindings with `pybind11`

`pybind11` is a modern library that makes it easy to expose C++ code to Python with minimal boilerplate.

- **Example**: Using `pybind11` to wrap C++ code:

1. **C++ Code (example.cpp)**:

```cpp
#include <pybind11/pybind11.h>

void say_hello() {
    std::cout << "Hello from C++!" << std::endl;
}

PYBIND11_MODULE(mylib, m) {
    m.def("say_hello", &say_hello, "A function that says hello");
}
```

2. **Compiling with `pybind11`**:

```bash
c++ -O3 -Wall -shared -std=c++11 -fPIC `python3 -m pybind11 --includes` example.cpp -o mylib`python3-config --extension-suffix`
```

3. **Python Code**:

```python
import mylib
mylib.say_hello()
```

16.2 Calling C++ Code from Java and .NET

C++ is often used in high-performance applications, and integrating it with Java and .NET allows developers to take advantage of existing ecosystems while maintaining performance.

16.2.1 Calling C++ from Java with JNI (Java Native Interface)

The **Java Native Interface (JNI)** is a framework that allows Java code to interact with C or C++ code. By using JNI, you can call C++ functions from Java, enabling performance-critical operations to be written in C++.

- **Example**: Calling a C++ function from Java using JNI.

1. **C++ Code (NativeCode.cpp):**

```cpp
#include <jni.h>
#include <iostream>
```

```
extern "C" JNIEXPORT void JNICALL
Java_HelloWorld_sayHello(JNIEnv      *env,
jobject obj) {
    std::cout << "Hello from C++!" <<
std::endl;
}
```

2. Java Code (HelloWorld.java):

java

```java
public class HelloWorld {
    static {
        System.loadLibrary("NativeCode");
// Load the C++ shared library
    }

    public native void sayHello();

    public static void main(String[] args)
{
        new HelloWorld().sayHello();   //
Call the C++ function
    }
}
```

3. Compiling and Running:

 o Compile C++ code to a shared library.

o   Use javac to compile the Java code and then run
it.

16.2.2 Calling C++ from .NET with C++/CLI

C++/CLI is a language extension for C++ that enables C++
to interact with .NET frameworks. It allows you to write
managed code (that interacts with the .NET runtime) and
unmanaged code (C++ code) together.

- **Example**: Calling C++ code from a C# application.

1. **C++/CLI Code**:

```cpp
// MyCppClass.cpp
#include "stdafx.h"
using namespace System;

public ref class MyCppClass {
public:
    void SayHello() {
        Console::WriteLine("Hello      from
C++!");
    }
};
```

217

2. **C# Code**:

```csharp
using System;

class Program {
    static void Main() {
        MyCppClass obj = new MyCppClass();
        obj.SayHello();
    }
}
```

3. **Compiling and Running**:
   o Use Visual Studio to build the C++/CLI project as a .NET assembly.
   o Reference this assembly in the C# project.

16.3 Using C++ in Web Development

C++ is increasingly being used in web development, especially in performance-critical areas. Two key areas where C++ plays a role in web development are **WebAssembly** and **server-side development**.

16.3.1 C++ and WebAssembly (Wasm)

WebAssembly (Wasm) allows you to run C++ code directly in the browser. It provides near-native performance, making it ideal for computationally intensive tasks in web applications.

- **Example**: Compiling C++ to WebAssembly.

1. **C++ Code (main.cpp)**:

cpp

```
#include <iostream>

int add(int a, int b) {
    return a + b;
}

int main() {
    std::cout << "Hello from WebAssembly!"
<< std::endl;
}
```

2. **Compiling with Emscripten**: Emscripten is a toolchain that compiles C++ code into WebAssembly.

```bash
emcc main.cpp -o main.js
```

3. **HTML/JavaScript to Call WebAssembly**:

```html
<script>
    var Module = {
        onRuntimeInitialized: function() {
            console.log("WebAssembly
loaded and initialized!");
            console.log("Result of add(2,
3): " + Module._add(2, 3));
        }
    };
</script>
<script src="main.js"></script>
```

16.3.2 C++ for Server-Side Development

C++ is used in server-side development where performance is crucial, such as in high-frequency trading, game servers, and large-scale distributed systems.

- **C++ Web Frameworks**:
    o **Crow**: A C++ web framework inspired by Python's Flask. It's lightweight and fast, making

220

it suitable for building REST APIs and web services in C++.

- o **CppCMS**: A high-performance C++ web development framework designed for creating dynamic websites with minimal latency.

- **Example**: Creating a simple REST API using Crow:

cpp

```
#include "crow_all.h"

int main() {
    crow::SimpleApp app;

    CROW_ROUTE(app, "/")([]() {
        return "Hello, C++ Web Server!";
    });

    app.port(18080).run();
}
```

16.4 Foreign Function Interfaces (FFI)

Foreign Function Interfaces (FFI) allow programs written in one language to call functions written in another language. In C++, you can use FFI to call functions from C, C++, or other languages like Python, Java, or Rust.

16.4.1 Using FFI with C

C is one of the most commonly used languages for creating FFIs due to its simple ABI (Application Binary Interface). C++ can call C functions via `extern "C"` declarations.

cpp

```cpp
extern "C" {
    void c_function();
}
```

16.4.2 FFI in C++ with Other Languages

You can use FFI libraries to call C++ functions from other languages. For instance, **SWIG (Simplified Wrapper and Interface Generator)** is a popular tool for generating wrapper code to allow C++ functions to be called from languages like Python, Java, and others.

- **Example**: Using SWIG to integrate C++ with Python:
    - Write a C++ interface file (e.g., `example.i`) and use SWIG to generate the wrapper code.
    - Compile the C++ code and wrapper code into a shared library.
    - Import and call the C++ code from Python.

Conclusion

In this chapter, we explored how to integrate C++ with other languages, including Python, Java, .NET, and web technologies like WebAssembly. By using tools like **JNI**, **C++/CLI**, **FFI**, and **SWIG**, you can take advantage of the strengths of different languages in your C++ projects. We also discussed using C++ in **web development** through technologies like **WebAssembly** and server-side frameworks. Integration with other languages enhances the flexibility of your applications, allowing you to leverage different ecosystems while maintaining the performance and control that C++ offers.

CHAPTER 17

ADVANCED C++ TOPICS

As C++ continues to evolve, new features and optimizations help developers write cleaner, more efficient, and portable code. This chapter explores some of the advanced C++ topics that are vital for experienced developers, including **C++20 and upcoming features**, **compiler optimizations**, **writing cross-platform C++ code**, and **handling platform-specific issues**.

17.1 C++20 and Upcoming Features

C++20 brings numerous improvements to the language, enhancing both performance and usability. It introduces new language features, libraries, and better integration with modern software development paradigms.

17.1.1 Concepts

One of the most important features introduced in C++20 is **concepts**. Concepts are predicates that specify the requirements for template parameters, making templates more expressive and easier to understand.

- **Example**: Defining a concept to restrict a template
  parameter to integral types:

cpp

```cpp
#include <concepts>
#include <iostream>

template <std::integral T>
T add(T a, T b) {
    return a + b;
}

int main() {
    std::cout << add(5, 10) << std::endl;   // Valid: 5 and 10 are integers
    // std::cout << add(5.5, 10.5) << std::endl; // Invalid: double is not an integral type
    return 0;
}
```

Concepts allow the compiler to provide more informative
error messages, helping developers catch errors at compile
time.

17.1.2 Ranges

C++20 introduces the **Ranges** library, which provides a more functional approach to working with sequences of data. It offers high-level abstractions for iterating over containers and performing common operations such as filtering, transforming, and reducing.

- **Example**: Using the `ranges` library to filter and transform a sequence:

cpp

```cpp
#include <ranges>
#include <vector>
#include <iostream>

int main() {
    std::vector<int> numbers = {1, 2, 3, 4, 5, 6};

    auto result = numbers
                    | std::views::filter([](int n) { return n % 2 == 0; })
                    | std::views::transform([](int n) { return n * 2; });

    for (int num : result) {
```

```
        std::cout << num << " ";   // Output: 4 8
12
    }

    return 0;
}
```

The Ranges library simplifies working with iterators and enables better readability and composition of data operations.

17.1.3 Coroutines

Coroutines were introduced in C++20 to simplify asynchronous programming. Coroutines allow you to write asynchronous code as if it were synchronous, improving readability and maintainability.

- **Example**: A simple coroutine that simulates an asynchronous operation:

cpp

```cpp
#include <iostream>
#include <coroutine>

struct SimpleTask {
    struct promise_type;
```

```
    using              handle_type              =
std::coroutine_handle<promise_type>;

    struct promise_type {
        SimpleTask get_return_object() { return
SimpleTask{handle_type::from_promise(*this)}; }
        std::suspend_never  initial_suspend()  {
return {}; }
        std::suspend_never       final_suspend()
noexcept { return {}; }
        void return_void() {}
        void        unhandled_exception()        {
std::exit(1); }
    };

    handle_type h;

    SimpleTask(handle_type h) : h(h) {}
    ~SimpleTask() { h.destroy(); }

    void run() {
        h();
    }
};

SimpleTask myCoroutine() {
    std::cout << "Start coroutine\n";
    co_return;
    std::cout << "End coroutine\n";
```

```
}

int main() {
    SimpleTask task = myCoroutine();
    task.run();  // Output: Start coroutine
                 //         End coroutine
    return 0;
}
```

Coroutines significantly simplify the syntax of asynchronous programming and enable writing more intuitive code for tasks such as network operations or long-running computations.

17.1.4 Other Features in C++20

- **Modules**: Introduced to replace header files with a more efficient and modular way of organizing code. This helps reduce compile times and improves encapsulation.
- **Calendar and Time Zone Library**: Provides better handling for date and time, including time zones and calendars.
- **Ranges** and `std::span`: For better handling of collections and slices of arrays.
- **Enhanced `constexpr`**: More features are available at compile time, including dynamic memory allocation and new library functions like `std::vector`.

17.1.5 Upcoming Features in C++23

While C++20 has introduced many changes, **C++23** is shaping up to continue this trend with features like:

- **Expanded `constexpr`**: More algorithms can be computed at compile time.
- **Pattern Matching**: A powerful tool for more readable code when working with data structures.
- **Better error handling**: The introduction of **expected** to simplify error handling without exceptions.

17.2 Compiler Optimizations and Behavior

Compilers in C++ are becoming increasingly sophisticated, offering many optimizations to improve the performance of your code. Understanding these optimizations can help you write faster and more efficient C++ code.

17.2.1 Common Compiler Optimizations

- **Inlining Functions**: The compiler can replace a function call with the actual code of the function, avoiding the overhead of a function call. This is especially useful for small functions that are called frequently.

    o **Example**: Use `inline` to suggest to the compiler that a function should be inlined.

cpp

```
inline int add(int a, int b) {
    return a + b;
}
```

- **Loop Unrolling**: The compiler can transform loops to reduce the number of iterations and increase efficiency by minimizing branching.

- **Constant Propagation and Folding**: Compilers can evaluate constant expressions at compile time, replacing them with their values.

- **Dead Code Elimination**: The compiler can remove code that is never executed or whose results are never used.

- **Link-Time Optimization (LTO)**: Allows the compiler to optimize across the entire program, rather than just within individual translation units, improving overall performance.

17.2.2 Compiler Behavior and Flags

Understanding and configuring the compiler's behavior can help you control the optimization process.

- **GCC/Clang Optimization Flags**:
  - `-O1`, `-O2`, `-O3`: These flags control the optimization level. `-O3` enables aggressive optimizations, but it may increase compilation time.
  - `-Ofast`: Allows aggressive optimizations, including those that may break strict standards compliance.
  - `-flto`: Enables link-time optimization.
  - **Example**:

    bash

    ```
    g++ -O2 -flto my_program.cpp -o
    my_program
    ```

17.2.3 Profile-Guided Optimization (PGO)

Profile-guided optimization allows you to compile and profile your code, then recompile it based on real-world usage patterns. This results in a more optimized program, especially for critical paths.

- **Steps**:

  1. Compile the program with instrumentation (-fprofile-generate).

  2. Run the program to collect profile data.

  3. Recompile with the collected data (-fprofile-use).

17.3 Writing Cross-Platform C++ Code

Writing cross-platform code ensures that your application can run on various operating systems (Windows, macOS, Linux) without significant changes. C++ allows you to write platform-independent code, but platform-specific issues still need to be addressed.

17.3.1 Using Platform-Abstraction Libraries

- **C++ Standard Library**: The C++ Standard Library offers many features that are platform-independent, such as containers, algorithms, input/output, and multithreading.

- **Boost**: Boost is a widely used C++ library that provides platform-independent utilities, such as file systems, networking, and threading.

- **Cross-Platform Build Systems**:

o **CMake**: CMake is a widely used tool that
generates platform-specific build files (e.g.,
Makefiles, Visual Studio projects).

o **Autotools**: Used primarily for Unix-like systems
to generate Makefiles.

17.3.2 Using Conditional Compilation

Sometimes, you need to write platform-specific code.
Preprocessor directives like `#ifdef` and `#if` are used to
include platform-specific headers or code.

- **Example**: Platform-specific code using preprocessor
directives:

cpp

```cpp
#ifdef _WIN32
#include <windows.h>
#elif __linux__
#include <unistd.h>
#endif

void platform_specific_function() {
#ifdef _WIN32
    // Windows-specific code
#elif __linux__
    // Linux-specific code
```

```
#endif
}
```

17.3.3 Cross-Platform GUI Libraries

For creating graphical user interfaces (GUIs) that work across different platforms, you can use libraries like:

- **Qt**: A popular cross-platform library for GUI applications.
- **wxWidgets**: Another cross-platform library for GUI development.

17.4 Handling Platform-Specific Issues

While C++ provides many ways to write cross-platform code, handling platform-specific issues often requires writing code that interacts with the operating system.

17.4.1 File System Differences

Different operating systems use different file system conventions:

- **Windows** uses backslashes (\) for file paths, while **Linux** and **macOS** use forward slashes (/).

- **C++17** introduces the `<filesystem>` library, which abstracts these differences and allows you to write portable code.

cpp

```cpp
#include <filesystem>
namespace fs = std::filesystem;

int main() {
    fs::path file_path = "some_file.txt";
    std::cout << file_path.generic_string() << std::endl;
    return 0;
}
```

17.4.2 Threading and Synchronization

Different platforms may have different threading models or synchronization primitives. The C++ Standard Library provides platform-independent threading functionality via `std::thread`, `std::mutex`, and `std::atomic`, but there may still be platform-specific differences to consider for fine-grained control.

- **Windows**: Windows uses its own threading model (`CreateThread`).

- **POSIX**: Linux and macOS use POSIX threads (`pthreads`).

Use `std::thread` and other synchronization features to abstract these differences.

Conclusion

In this chapter, we explored several **advanced C++ topics** that are essential for experienced developers. We discussed **C++20 features**, including concepts, ranges, coroutines, and other improvements. We also covered **compiler optimizations** and how they impact performance, as well as best practices for writing **cross-platform C++ code** and handling **platform-specific issues**. By leveraging these advanced techniques and tools, you can write more efficient, portable, and modern C++ applications that work seamlessly across different platforms and use cases.

CHAPTER 18

REAL-WORLD C++ PROJECTS

In this chapter, we will explore several real-world applications of C++ in large-scale projects, including building a **game engine**, creating a **high-performance database engine**, working with an **existing large C++ codebase**, and examining **future trends in C++ development**. These examples will demonstrate how C++ is used in complex, performance-critical software and highlight key strategies for handling such large projects.

18.1 Building a Game Engine

Building a game engine is one of the most challenging and rewarding projects you can undertake as a C++ developer. A game engine is responsible for rendering graphics, handling physics, managing assets, processing input, and more. A good game engine is highly modular, flexible, and optimized for performance.

18.1.1 Key Components of a Game Engine

1. **Rendering Engine**: This component manages how
   objects and scenes are drawn to the screen. It
   interacts with APIs like OpenGL, DirectX, or Vulkan
   to handle graphics rendering.

   o **Example**: A basic rendering engine using
   OpenGL:

cpp

```cpp
void render() {
    glClear(GL_COLOR_BUFFER_BIT         |
GL_DEPTH_BUFFER_BIT);
    glLoadIdentity();
    glTranslatef(0.0f, 0.0f, -5.0f);
    // Draw objects here
    glFlush();
}
```

2. **Physics Engine**: Handles the movement and
   interaction of objects in a simulated environment. It
   may include features like collision detection, rigid
   body dynamics, and gravity.

   o **Example**: A simple physics update for objects:

cpp

```cpp
struct Object {
    float x, y, z;
    float velocityX, velocityY, velocityZ;
};

void updatePhysics(Object& obj, float
deltaTime) {
    obj.x += obj.velocityX * deltaTime;
    obj.y += obj.velocityY * deltaTime;
    obj.z += obj.velocityZ * deltaTime;
}
```

3. **Asset Management**: The game engine needs to load, manage, and organize assets (textures, models, sounds). This system needs to be efficient for both loading and memory management.

   o **Example**: A basic asset manager might load a texture:

cpp

```cpp
GLuint loadTexture(const std::string&
filename) {
    GLuint textureID;
    glGenTextures(1, &textureID);
    glBindTexture(GL_TEXTURE_2D,
textureID);
```

```
// Load texture image and set
parameters here
    return textureID;
}
```

4. **Input System**: The input system manages user input from devices like the keyboard, mouse, and game controllers. It translates raw input into actions in the game world.

   o **Example**: Handling basic keyboard input using SDL (Simple DirectMedia Layer):

cpp

```cpp
if (SDL_PollEvent(&event)) {
    if (event.type == SDL_QUIT) {
        exit(0);
    }
    if (event.type == SDL_KEYDOWN) {
        if    (event.key.keysym.sym    ==
SDLK_ESCAPE) {
            // Pause or exit game
        }
    }
}
```

5. **Audio Engine**: Plays sound effects and background music. This can be handled through libraries like OpenAL or FMOD.

   o **Example**: Playing a sound using OpenAL:

cpp

```
ALuint soundBuffer, soundSource;
alGenBuffers(1, &soundBuffer);
alBufferData(soundBuffer,
AL_FORMAT_MONO16,    soundData,    dataSize,
sampleRate);
alGenSources(1, &soundSource);
alSourcei(soundSource,          AL_BUFFER,
soundBuffer);
alSourcePlay(soundSource);
```

18.1.2 Performance Considerations

Building a game engine involves constant optimization for real-time performance. Key considerations include:

- **Multithreading**: Offload non-graphics work (e.g., physics, AI) to separate threads to maximize CPU usage.
- **Memory Management**: Efficiently manage memory, use memory pools, and minimize allocations during gameplay.

- **Level of Detail (LOD)**: Reduce the complexity of distant objects to save processing power.
- **Culling**: Use techniques like frustum and occlusion culling to avoid rendering objects that are out of view or blocked.

18.1.3 Tools and Libraries for Game Development

- **Game Engines**: You can either build a custom engine from scratch or use existing engines like **Unreal Engine** (C++-based) or **Unity** (using C++ for core development).
- **Libraries**: OpenGL, SDL, Vulkan, Bullet (for physics), and FMOD are commonly used in custom game engine development.

18.2 Creating a High-Performance Database Engine

Database engines are the backbone of systems that need to store, manage, and retrieve large volumes of data efficiently. Writing a high-performance database engine in C++ requires a deep understanding of indexing, query optimization, and concurrency management.

18.2.1 Key Components of a Database Engine

1. **Storage Engine**: The storage engine is responsible for persisting data to disk and retrieving it when

necessary. C++ is well-suited for implementing efficient storage systems.

- o **Example**: A simple key-value store might use a hash table for in-memory storage:

cpp

```
std::unordered_map<std::string,
std::string> db;
db["user1"] = "password123";
db["user2"] = "password456";
```

2. **Query Processor**: The query processor interprets SQL or custom queries and converts them into operations on the storage engine. This includes query parsing, optimization, and execution.

- o **Example**: A basic query processor might parse a simple SQL query and execute it:

cpp

```
std::string query = "SELECT * FROM users";
if (query == "SELECT * FROM users") {
    // Execute the query
}
```

3. **Indexing**: Database engines often use B-trees or other indexing techniques to speed up search operations.

   o **Example**: Implementing a simple index using a map:

cpp

```cpp
std::map<int, std::string> userIndex;
userIndex[1001] = "user1";
userIndex[1002] = "user2";
```

4. **Transaction Management**: A database engine must support ACID (Atomicity, Consistency, Isolation, Durability) properties to ensure data integrity during transactions.

   o **Example**: Using C++ to manage a transaction:

cpp

```cpp
bool beginTransaction() {
    // Start a new transaction
    return true;
}

bool commitTransaction() {
    // Commit the transaction
    return true;
```

```
    }

    bool rollbackTransaction() {
        // Rollback the transaction
        return false;
    }
```

18.2.2 Performance Considerations

- **Concurrency Control**: Use locking or optimistic concurrency control techniques to allow multiple transactions to happen concurrently without data corruption.
- **Indexing**: Use efficient indexing structures, such as B-trees or hash indexes, to speed up data retrieval.
- **Write-Ahead Logging (WAL)**: A technique to ensure durability by writing changes to a log before updating the main database.

18.2.3 Tools and Libraries

- **Libraries**: SQLite (a lightweight database engine), LevelDB, and RocksDB (for key-value stores).
- **Tools**: Profiling tools like **Valgrind** and **gprof** are essential for identifying performance bottlenecks in database engines.

18.3 Working with an Existing Large C++ Codebase

Working with a large, existing C++ codebase can be challenging due to its complexity and scale. Understanding how to navigate, refactor, and optimize large C++ projects is key to maintaining and improving them.

18.3.1 Navigating the Codebase

- **Modular Design**: Ensure that the codebase is modular, with clear boundaries between components or subsystems. This makes it easier to work on specific parts of the code without affecting other areas.
- **Documentation**: Ensure that the code is well-documented. Use **Doxygen** or other tools to generate documentation from comments.
- **Code Navigation Tools**: Use IDEs like CLion, Visual Studio, or VSCode with advanced search and code navigation features to quickly locate relevant files and functions.

18.3.2 Refactoring and Code Quality

- **Refactoring**: Regularly refactor the code to improve readability, maintainability, and performance. Break large functions into smaller ones and simplify complex logic.

247

- **Code Reviews**: Conduct regular code reviews to ensure high-quality code and consistency.
- **Static Analysis**: Use static analysis tools like **Cppcheck** or **Clang Static Analyzer** to detect potential issues early.

18.3.3 Dependency Management

Managing dependencies is critical for large projects. Use **CMake** for managing builds and dependencies across multiple platforms. Consider using dependency management tools like **Conan** or **vcpkg** for handling third-party libraries.

18.4 Future Trends in C++ Development

The C++ language continues to evolve, and several trends will shape its future:

18.4.1 C++ and Parallelism

As multi-core processors become more common, parallelism is a growing area of focus for C++. Future versions of C++ will likely include more abstractions and libraries to simplify writing parallel code. C++20 introduced **std::jthread** for easier threading management.

18.4.2 Modern C++ Practices

The trend toward **modern C++** practices emphasizes:

- **Automatic memory management** with smart pointers (`std::unique_ptr`, `std::shared_ptr`).
- **Type safety** using **concepts** and **type traits**.
- **Immutability** and **functional programming** approaches.

18.4.3 C++ and Machine Learning

With the rise of machine learning, C++ is becoming more prevalent in this field due to its performance advantages. Libraries like **TensorFlow** and **MLPack** are written in C++ for performance-critical tasks.

18.4.4 Tooling Improvements

The C++ tooling ecosystem is continuously improving with better IDEs, debuggers, and build systems. Tools like **Clangd** and **CMake** continue to evolve, making it easier to work with C++ projects.

Conclusion

In this chapter, we explored several **real-world C++ projects**, from building a **game engine** to creating a **high-**

performance database engine. We discussed the challenges of working with an **existing large C++ codebase** and highlighted **future trends in C++ development**. These examples demonstrate C++'s versatility and its critical role in high-performance software development, and as the language continues to evolve, it will remain an essential tool for developers across various industries.